Sound is movement of air. ... winds of thought, whirlwinds of beauty, ... intently, imagine courageously, and hear it.

Ray Hughes
Selah Ministries, www.selahministries.com

Your heart will burn within you, as mine did, when you read *Can You Hear the Sound?* by Donna Milham. Holy Spirit's words through Donna's pen will cut to the depths of your soul with truth and power clothed in beauty and grace. Every word resonates with the frequency of heaven and with notes from the Father's heart. Every poem calls out, spirit to spirit, deep to deep, drawing us into realms of eternity that are found only in Him. As revelation flows, Donna, like a master craftsman, paints an earthly picture of a heavenly reality, revealing God's beauty and drawing us into His arms. This is not a book to be read once and forgotten, but to feast upon again and again.

Virginia Killingsworth
All Things Restored, www.virginiakillingsworth.com, www.allthingsrestored.org

I am honored to be able to say a little about Donna Milham and *Can You Hear the Sound?* Donna is not a long-time "natural" acquaintance or friend. Upon first meeting, I recognized "a sister in the kinship of His Spirit" in her. Being women of prayer, worship, and the prophetic gave us grounds for mutuality, but it was not until I stepped into the pages of her book that I began to encounter her. I must confess that some of its pages seemed like whispered echoes of my own journals. But the phrases that flowed from the essence of her spirit took me deeper, higher, and nearer than my own glimpses had allowed me to go. His Spirit through Donna's spirit aroused buried creative facets in me that had fallen into slumber or been stopped in their gestational development and were withering away. She brought resurrection's breath to fill my soul's empty sails. I was awakened as one who had almost slept herself into amnesia. *Can You Hear the Sound's* poetic yet practical words, like gentle goads, pressed me back to Father's life path for me. Donna has a unique ability to hear what others cannot yet perceive and respond to it with wholehearted obedience. Like a dog at its Master's hand, she lives out those higher sounds that are outside of the average worshiper's hearing. I have been given the privilege to be awakened and taught by a teacher who carries the scars of cross-tried love. I hope you will be as transformed by these chronicles of that love as I have been.

Christine Potter
Potterhaus Music, www.potterhausmusic.net

Like a drum sounding through the silence of a winter's night, Donna Milham's book, *Can You Hear the Sound?*, brings a clear call to hungry hearts wanting to find and fulfill the destiny chosen for them from the foundations of the earth. This is an invitation into the adventure of a life of one who lives for no one but Jesus. The poetic flow reminds me of a psalmist in tune with the nuances of God. The book leads you to a place of turning pages, once unwritten, but pages that needed to be written as God calls you onward. Like an artistic scribe, Donna asks the questions that draw you closer to Jesus and, in the same breath, asks the questions that reveal your heart. The challenge is real; Donna has lived that. But it's the drawing of the Lord into the rest that He gives in those experiences that provides the answers to those challenges.

The passionate imagery in the book is a mark of creativity that this generation greatly desires. "Love flashing like a fiery inferno—bursting forth vibrant flames." Brilliant words on empty pages expressing the heart of a lover of Jesus. I have known Donna for a long time. I've witnessed her heart passionately beating on a drum, sounding through a voice, or encouraging the broken. I've seen a warrior and a lover; I've watched her break and I've watched her rise. The skill of knowing the instrument on which she plays is amazing. It's not what most think it is. She plays the notes, the sounds of the breath of God, through the demonstration of her life. As you read this book, you will find there is an instrument you never knew could be played on the heartstrings of your very being. Donna just played them. Can you hear the sounds?

Danny Steyne
Mountain of Worship, www.mountainofworship.com

Can You Hear *the* Sound?

Releasing the Sound of the Heartbeat of
God through Revelatory Writings

Donna Milham

Published by
Constant Hope Publishing,
a division of Connie Scott Productions
www.ConnieScott.com

ISBN-13: 978-0-578-41453-9
(previously ISBN-13: 978-1942056508)

Library of Congress Control Number: 2017945640

Can You Hear the Sound?: Releasing the Sound of the Heartbeat of God through Revelatory Writings

Photographer: Andrea Van Boven (Multifacetblog.net)

Printed in the USA.

Contents

Foreword   7

Introduction   9

Chapter One: Can You Hear the Sound?   11
Can You Hear the Sound of Let My People Go That They May Worship Me?   11
Can You Hear the Sound of Divine Possession?   14
Can You Hear the Sound of the King of Glory?   19
Can You Hear the Sound of the Page Turning in Heaven?   24
Can You Hear the Sound of the Page Turning in Your Life?   27
Emmaus Road—Can You Hear the Sound of Hearts Burning within Us?   30
The Sound of Ten Healed of Leprosy   31
Can You Hear Me Now?   36

Chapter Two: The Sound of Resurrection   39
The Sound of Weeping at His Feet   39
Can You Hear the Sound of the Stone Being Rolled Away?   41
Sounds of Resurrection   43
Awaken the Dawn with the Song of Resurrection Life   44
The Sound of Stones Being Rolled Away   45
The Sound of Resurrection's Release   47
Can You Hear the Sound of His Blood Still Dripping?   49

Chapter Three: The Sound of Awakeners   51
Sounds above and on Earth   51
The Sound of the Woman Bursting Forth into the Room   52
The Sound of Dawn Awakeners   53
Awakening the Night   53
Good Morning, Dawn   55
Encounter—Songs of Awakening—Songs of Light   60

Chapter Four: The Sound of Personal Encounter   65
Can You Hear the Sound of Peace?   65
Where Is the Sound of His Finger Writing?   65
Where Is the Sound of the Holy Kiss of Heaven?   66
Do You Hear the Sound of Birthing?   66

Womb of the Dawn   68
The Sound of Women Being Set Free   70
The Sound of Women Arising   70

Chapter Five: The Sound Of Belonging and Sonship   **71**
Can You Hear the Sound of Authority?   71
The Sound of His Glad Welcome   73
Can You Hear the Sound of His Songs of Gladness over You?   75

Chapter Six: Can You Hear the Sound of the Father's Voice?   **77**

Chapter Seven: Mary's Prophetic Song and Sounds   **81**

Chapter Eight: Can You Hear the Sound of His Kingdom Authority?   **91**
Dominion's Sound   91
The God of Glory Thunders   92
The Sound of His Blood and His Love   97
Unstoppable Ones   98
The Sound of Holy Impregnation Is upon Us   102
Hear His Roar of Glory   103

Chapter Nine: The Sound of the Eternal One   **105**
What Love Is This?   105
A Baby's Cry—A Lion's Roar   108
Hear the Sound of the Keys of Dominion Authority   110
Eternity's Pulse of Worship   112
Sound of the Immortal Seed Within   114

Chapter Ten: The Sound of New Creation   **121**
Can You Hear the Sound of a New Man—A New Race?   121
Silence in the Garden   124
Can You Hear the Sound of Goodness and Mercy?   126
Do You Hear the Sound of a Door Open: Come Up Here?   128

Chapter Eleven: The Sound of Forgiveness   **129**
Breathe Out, Breathe In—Can You Hear the Sound of His Breath?   129
Can You Hear the Sound of Forgiveness?   130

Foreword

There is a wooing from heaven to come up above the noise of this world and hear the sound of heaven. The Father has been calling sons and daughters to lean into His heart and hear His heartbeat. His longing for His children to be in tune with His heart frequency has been resounding from heaven into earth.

Donna Milham is a forerunner in the body of Christ in arts and sound. She has been hearing and releasing the sound of the Father's heart for close to two decades. Her words resonate with the sound of heaven. Her compilation of revelatory writings in *Can You Hear the Sound?* resonates with the Father's heartbeat. Each thought, each page, each piece revealing His love for His children. The harmony of His love is felt as you turn the pages. The Father's desire is to silence every discordant noise in our lives so the sound of His voice is heard.

Donna is one who is compelled to go up the mountain of the Lord, to encounter the One who continues to awaken her heart to His. She follows Him wherever He may lead, laying down her life to be His friend, His voice, and His scribe. Donna lives to reveal the beauty of who He is. Sometimes it is a lonely journey as she has counted the cost of being misunderstood. Yet I know she considers it worth it all if just one life is touched, awakened, and transformed. I have seen the revelation the Lord gives her awaken and transform many.

I love exquisite organic dark chocolate, but I never eat it all in one sitting. I enjoy it one piece at a time, often sitting with a cup of organic green tea, in the moment savoring the aromas and flavors. This collection of revelatory writings is like that to me. I encourage you to find a quiet space, be still, and savor these sweet and strong truths as you listen for the voice of your Beloved.

Donna writes of the sound of transforming love. She calls out to those who will be prisoners of love, releasing the "Sound of Hope—The Sound of Forgiveness." These sounds will transform you. She invites you to encounter the sound of the Father's fountains of grace. These life-giving messages are invitations to experience the One whose sound brings true peace.

Donna has heard and declares the Father's voice as He calls out, "They are mine!" She has heard the shackles of the enemy's lies come off her own life. In the pages of this book, she releases these encounters with His voice to you, the reader, so you too can be free to become who God says you are.

As you turn the pages of these stunning revelations, may you turn away from hopelessness and turn to a life releasing hope found among the sounds of these words scribed from the Father's heart. May your heart align with the powerful sound of surrender, which Christ Jesus demonstrated when He came and lived as a mere man among us. His abandonment to the Father's voice caused dead bones to come together and a movement to arise that is still releasing His sound today.

Donna cries out to the Father, "Open our ear gates, Lord." May we join this cry and hear the sound of His heartbeat.

Living in the sound of His loving heartbeat,

Tracee Anne Loosle
Founder, Intrepid Heart Ministries & Abundance Center
www.intrepidheartministries.com

Introduction

The Lord whispered an invitation to my heart: Will you begin to walk the streets of this city and pray, pray My heart's longings?

I had been busy traveling and my vision had begun to turn to the nations. I felt His burden for this city, this island I live on, and my heart responded—yes!

I began to walk and pray, alone or with a friend, listening, decreeing, praying, worshiping. Sometimes I felt led to sit and wait silently with Him and listen in the Spirit. The Spirit of God led me to a part of the city I had not explored before. I found a wooden bench in a small neighborhood park overlooking the harbor and felt impressed to sit and wait.

As I sat there, suddenly I heard His voice, saying, "Will you give me a landing strip?" I waited, I pondered, and I said yes, I will, but please tell me what that means. To me a landing strip was a place for a plane to land. He responded, "It is a place prepared for Me to come and remain. I do not want to just visit—I want an abode, a place to dwell and stay."

Again I said yes, but please show me how. He shared with me that His eye was on this city and His heart longed for the people who lived here. He asked me to release the sound of His jealous roar, for His heart was filled with a holy, jealous love for each one and the people would come to the sound of His roar of this love. They would respond to the sound of home—their eternal home—where each one came from—the very heart of God!

He said, "Each one is Mine—no one else will own them. Release the sound—they will come."

So began the journey, the assignment to bring the One I love His heart's desire. All are His offspring but not yet His children; release the sound of His heartbeat of love!

Each time it is different, never the same, but it powerfully impacts and transforms my life.

The sounds are of another realm—the realm of holy divine love and all of its glory and splendor.

Can You Hear the Sound? is a compilation of this journey with the Holy Three—Father, Son, and Holy Spirit—and it continues, a never ending journey, now and for all eternity.

Chapter One: Can You Hear the Sound?

Can You Hear the Sound of Let My People Go That They May Worship Me?

Do you see the holy frenzy of a mountainside of worshipers?
All ages and sizes—some with instruments and some with dance.
Some have paintings strapped to their backs;
Some with dance shoes tied at their waists.
Others with sculpting tools in pouches on their sides,
Some with cameras for scenes they are watching
And waiting to unfold,
Some hold pens with feathers of white and gold attached,
For pure and holy revelation to scribe and record.
Some with books as scrolls around their necks and over their hearts,
Poems penned in hours of passion with their King.
Can you see it?
It's not very orderly to the world,
But the King sees and His heart is bursting at the sight.
These have been accused, abused, beaten, misunderstood, laughed at,
ridiculed, hated, despised, scorned and yet arise—
They get up and worship,
They won't be stopped.
His love, His fiery love compels them—ever up, ever up the mountain,
The mountain of holy desire, the mountain of fiery love,
The mountain of consuming.
Knowing at the top awaits the altar of sacrifice, altar of worship,
Laying the offerings of heartfelt devotion
At His feet
And watching them be consumed in His love.

And there is the pinnacle of all life—
Fulfilling His heart's desires, giving Him pleasure.
And what is one's response? You fall at His feet in worship;

Can You Hear the Sound?

You fall at His feet in gratitude.
The I AM—the One who was and is and is to come—
Has embraced all you are;
That which others may have rejected, He has received,
And you fall in wonder upon your face and
Kiss His feet of peace,
Strengthening even more the resolve within—
To love Him radically and war against anything
That would try to hold you back from total expression
Of holy passion to the Lover of your soul,
To the Holy One worthy to be worshiped and adored.

With fresh impartation of holy peace to defeat the lies,
Defeat the enemies of lavished worship—
Down the mountain you go,
Focused and fixed in heart, soul, and spirit,
Looking for others to join in the next climb up the mountain of visitation.
You walk the earth with His cry in your heart,
Resounding like a trumpet call:
Let His people go that they may worship Him!
The cry rings out, blares out from a place so deep within,
Shaking your very core—
It is the cry of the King who lives within you,
The Deliverer within you,
For the mountain of worship is freedom for all who ascend.
Will you answer the call up the mountain?
Not in a perfect line of man's prescribed ways
But in the unique and diverse expressions of true worship—
Abandoned and reckless—
For those who worship Him must do so in spirit and in truth.
Will you ascend the mountain of visitation
With your offerings of worship—
Expecting to meet Him,
Expecting transformation,
Expecting acceptance,

Expecting impartation,
Expecting pierced feet that made the way for you to climb
His holy mountain,
Feet that gave you access—pierced for you?
Will you leave the familiar, comfortable paradigm of worship
And venture higher?
He's waiting for you there.
Do you hear the trumpet blaring out from His heart?
"Let my people go, so they can worship me" (Exodus 8:1 NLT).
He breaks you free this day and calls you up to ascend into Him!

Can You Hear the Sound of Divine Possession?

A sound is coming—hear it and then release it.

The sound of the movement of the King,
The sound of wind and fire,
The sound of His breath—
Breath of life, breath of fire—
Imparting and consuming,
Empowering and overtaking,
Whirlwind of His fiery presence,
Consummation of the Divine Three
  Upon us
To consume and to saturate and to possess
A people to be flames of fire
Who know His breath of life
  That keeps the flame burning,
Gladly offering self as fuel—an object of fiery blaze—
Not burned, but consumed and purified.
  Gold and holiness,
Not right and wrong,
  Not the Tree of the Knowledge of Good and Evil,
But from divine union—God in us—His life,
His life lived through us,
Peaceful, rest, quiet, still,
  Saturating love,
Great possessor of our souls.
As we give access to the Great Liberator and Great Possessor,
Endless cycle of activity ceases;
Activity is one of surrender and abandonment
For His heart's desire
And His kingdom.
Throne within His heart,

His throne within our hearts,
One King—one kingdom,
One Lord—one purpose.
Fear of death must go—
        Death of self,
        Death of self-dreams,
        Death of being known,
        Death of men's ways and approval,
        Physical death—death of anything except Him living in us.
Then we know true freedom,
Fear has lost its grip and hold.
What can we lose?
        Reputation—not to seek one,
        Man's recognition—seek only heaven's,
        Physical life—we go to be with Him in heaven.
Journey into Him—the depths of the chambers of life Himself;
Way and truth lead into Him—union with Him.
Not just being with God,
But we live and move and have our being in Him.
Divine mystery, mysteries and secrets,
Hidden life, whether physically visible or hidden away,
We are hidden in Him—He lives through us.
All music, art, dance, sound—creativity,
Releasing Him, revealing Him and His nature and character—
Holy display of awestruck splendor and brilliance of a wondrous God,
Joyous God, confident God, glad God,
        Tender and terrible,
        Good and righteous Judge.
Participate with all creation and reveal Him
And Jesus Christ revealed through us.
This is the purpose that the arts are now being restored,
Not to be known, but that He will be seen and be known and worshiped.
Time for reverence and awe to return,
Passion and purity and radiance,
His power and His grace, His might and His mercy,

His depths and His glories,
Cutting ties that keep us bound to earth's shores,
And allow us to journey into the depths of the mysteries of Christ.
Navigators of His heart,
Going in and coming out and showing the way and truth and life,
Where all color and sound and creation come from
Light—light of divine God,
Holy Three yet one.
        Mystery of mysteries,
Encompassing of the triune God,
Enfolding us into Their very nature and being
That we would be sons and daughters of the King,
Whose steps are one with Him, and heaven moves with us,
Watching, ever watching those who have given up much to get all of Him.
        Known in heaven,
Hidden within His very self,
God in man—hidden in Him,
The power of this and yet the simplicity of abandonment,
Courage to give up, give way for holy habitation.
He woos us with the shepherd's flute—come home into My heart,
Come into eternity's chambers where for all time it will unfold revelation
After revelation after revelation,
Never to be exhausted and we are to live "there"—now,
Where "there" is more real than here.
Then we are aliens of earth and earth's kingdoms—we live seated in
heavenly places with Him.
This becomes more and more a reality to us,
Until His shadow—His manifest presence—is actually covering us,
surrounding us,
Tabernacles, habitations, individual temples,
Together, corporately releasing His wonders.
Why do we try to echo each other?
Let us echo heaven and its choruses, its angel songs, its dialogues,
Its songs back and forth—elders and cherubim and saints and seraphim;
Let us resound and echo heaven on earth.

Let us be the clear clarion sound.
For all of time we will worship and fall down
As He unfolds another facet of Himself
And the angelic hosts rejoice with the saints.
Can this not begin now?
Explosions of light and color,
Sound, movement, shape
Being released through us, to us, to earth
To show Jesus Christ and the reality of heaven,
The revelation of throne realm activity,
Not performance and accolades,
But revealing our true home—the Father's house.
Kingdom realm reality, far surpassing our own ability to perceive;
Holy Spirit, Teacher and Guide, reveals and leads us into truth Himself.
Open door—Revelation 4—access:
Come up here!
Live and see from this reality,
Splendor beams escaping now,
Time of access is here for those who will throw off
Earth's weights and affection,
To be able to ascend in their heart and spirit,
Throwing off every distraction
To arise and go up into the heights of heavenly places.
Just when you think this can't be true, this is too far out there,
You hear again
The shepherd's flute beckoning you to the narrow way,
The way of the mystical saints—the way of Jesus, the mystical priest,
The way of the beloved.
Breath of songs of the saints
Echoes through time—surrounding, passing around and through,
His breath released,
Creating—galaxy upon galaxy—
Ever enlarging;
His breath is being released to encircle and enlarge and expand
The territory of our hearts and spirits,

The wide expanse of His reality—His kingdom and His home.
Voices today mingle with echoes of yesterday's song;
Waves of divine love and passion being released, washing over us,
Laying on the sands of time,
In the position of the cross—glad surrender.
In this holiest of moments, we gladly let all go with the waves,
Carrying away pieces of self in exchange for more of Him.
Overtaking—overtaking,
Sounds around you become sounds within you;
Heaven's song is now within.
We don't struggle to let go of things—
The smallest thing that doesn't resemble Him,
We long and seek to let it melt away in His fiery gaze of love,
In His presence of light,
In His passionate embrace of words of love.
He wraps us in a blanket of proclamation of "future and hope"
And in this safety and promise by the One who cannot lie,
        We say yes.
Here we are; take us far deeper than ever,
Send us, for He cannot send us out as His ambassadors of His heart
Until He can have us fully.
Holy takeover—
A takeover of every wound, every sorrow, every sadness,
Every disappointment, every hurt, every broken promise.
A takeover—to take you in and then send you out;
You go in and go out and go in and go out;
You scribe, sing, dance, paint, sculpt, write—
Release what you hear, see, experience with Him, in Him.
His seal is on it and men's hearts are moved by His heart uncovered;
Man has not rejected Jesus—man has rejected religion.
Will we be the ones to give them the chance
For their five senses to be awakened so they can choose eternal life?

Can You Hear the Sound of the King of Glory?

Psalms 24:8

He rises from His throne and steps through time and space.
He walks through galaxies, inspecting each He has placed by His hand—
Each named and declaring His wonders, His radiant splendor,
Each star illuminating the brightness of His character—
His very nature is light.
He steps through constellations—
King of glory.
He stops and whispers to Earth,
"Look up and see nature declaring who I AM!
I am the Lord, mighty in battle.
Each step I take in the heavenlies I leave a footprint of light;
Swirling light and the heavenly host follow Me in holy array.
You call them the northern lights,
But they are My host surrounding Me—with Me—
As I walk through the heavens.
Divine light explosions—
My steps—from My feet of light,
Bright brilliant light and stars shoot across the sky."
They shoot in jubilant wonder and praise;
The Creator is passing by—they can't remain in place.
They are messengers of "He is on the move."
Let Me light the path in the first heaven—
Let me open your eyes today to see
Paths of brilliant light as I go before you,
The God of light,
Lighting the path to the highway of holiness,
Highway of the beauty realm of My beauty,
Highway of My majestic realm,
Highway of radiating glory and light.
See the nail scars in My feet;

See the light beams radiating out—
  Resurrection,
    Resurrection,
      Resurrection
        Light, life, power.
Mary kissed, washed, anointed the feet of God made flesh;
Mary watched them bleed on the cross—red drops of mercy—
  Feet that descended and ascended
  Arose to be seated at the right hand of the Father,
  Brilliant flashing feet at His throne,
Victorious feet radiating peace,
  Crushing, powerful peace,
  Deathblow feet.
  What can bear the weight of eternity's feet?
  What could stop their crushing weight of might?
Yes those feet gladly, willingly submitted to take our sins,
  To be nailed.
  Two feet—one nail.
  Total submission of His walk and His way,
  Rendering dead the flesh
And walking in our own understandings, plans, and paths.
Oh, run to the foot of the cross;
Kiss the feet—nail-pierced feet.
Worship His obedience;
Worship His sacrifice;
Worship both feet given in holy submission
That at His feet our lives
  Captured by such a love act
  Would say
  Pierce both of my feet, Lord,
  With Your love nails
  Drive them into every place of my independent life and walk;
  Cause me to follow You
  Every step, every day.

Donna Milham

Feet that dance,
Dancing feet—over you!
Feet that celebrated the disciples' victory
As Satan fell like lightning from the sky,
As their feet walked in His plan and will;
Feet that dance and leap in joy and delight
That you are His.
Why else did He hang on that cross?
He looked down the halls of eternity and saw Himself
Dancing for you and with you.
He hung there, knowing He would dance with you, dance over you.
Feet that dance and leap in joy and celebration—
You are His promise,
You are His passion.
The passionate loving One, loving you to death.
He loves us to the death of ourselves,
He loves the flesh out of us,
He loves fear out of us,
He loves envy out of us,
He loves seeking man's recognition out of us,
He loves shame out of us,
He loves self-hatred out of us,
He loves unworthiness out of us.
Dancing feet, prophesying value, worth, honor, greatness, esteem,
blessing.
Dancing feet of joy, spinning and leaping—
Whirlwind of love around you.
Step out of the whirlwind of the enemy and into the whirlwind of His love.
Let it envelop you and overtake you and let it catch you up and in,
For in this whirlwind are the feet of fire that belong to the
Burning man—Christ Jesus,
Burning red hot for you.
Feet—blazing fiery feet,
Footsteps of fire
Leading to the altar of sacrificial love.

Moses took that path—a fiery path with fiery footprints—
Alone,
To meet with the burning God—the burning bush.
As we walk the path of burning fire,
Slowly hay, wood, and stubble is consumed;
A slow inner burning—
      Burning man, burning feet,
      Working deep within,
All the way to the altar of burning desire,
Consuming altar of divine exchange,
Feet that drip oil
      On the foreheads
      Of those waiting at His cross,
      Offering their lives as living sacrifices.
Drip, drip, drip, drip, drip,
      Dripping grace
To embrace the crucified life
      That from your feet oil may come forth,
      Leaving scented, fragrant paths that lead to Him.
Do you smell the myrrh?
      The paths of myrrh,
      The costly path;
Feet that walked on water.
The one who spoke oceans into existence and set their boundaries
Now walked on them;
Feet that contain and that hold
All power and all might,
They resound in majesty with each step,
Releasing roaring waves of might.
Tsunami waves coming,
Tsunami waves coming
To overtake, to overtake;
Tsunami waves of extravagant love to overtake you,
Overwhelm you,
With all-encompassing waters of love.

Lost in the sea of His love,
Deep calling unto deep,
Deep ocean depths of His love.
If you get close to His feet you can hear the waves in the nail-scarred feet,
Waves of love,
Governmental love commanding seas,
      Commanding our lives—if we give way.
We cry out in the storms;
      He crosses the sea,
      He gets into the boat,
      He speaks to the sea;
      Instantly we are on the other side of our circumstance.
      From the shore of the familiar
      To the sea of the unknown
      To the shore of promise, future, hope.

Can You Hear the Sound of the Page Turning in Heaven?

Can you hear the sound of the page turning in heaven?
The Glorious One has taken off His royal garments;
He has stepped out of heaven.
He has stepped into the womb of a humble servant on earth
In the form of a seed.
Once in the heavens,
Now on earth,
Humility at its highest peak:
A King became a seed in a womb
To purchase men's hearts for His Father.

Who can imagine, envision such a plan, a strategy, a scheme?
Only the heart of a passionate Father longing for His own,
Only a Son who lives for His Father's pleasure.
Only He would step down,
Leaving all divinity,
Becoming a man.

Can you hear the sound of the page turning?
What was it like in heaven when He stepped out?
What was it like on earth
When creation realized their creator had come down?
Was there silence in heaven?
Was there praise on earth?

Can you hear the sound of the page turning
As Mary's life is changed forever,
As her womb is impregnated with the promise
That would bring forth the Promise for all mankind?
She carried Him within her womb,
The salvation of mankind,

Greatest honor of all time.
He chose a simple lover's heart and womb,
A devoted one.

Can you hear the sound of the page turning?
He's turned the tables upside down in the temple;
He's healed blind eyes, raised the dead, cast out demons,
Preached the kingdom of God is at hand.
He's touched the lepers, embraced the prostitutes, eaten with sinners;
He's confronted the Pharisees and delivered the demoniac,
Their lives changed forever.

Can you hear the sound of the page turning
As death, hell, and the grave are defeated forever?
"Father, forgive them,
For they don't know what they're doing" (Luke 23:34).
Death is swallowed up in victory, holy vacuum.
Consumed, no longer exists for those who are His own.
Eternity in heaven a reality—blood bought, costly price,
The One who stepped down now ascends.

Can you hear the sound of the page turning?
Descended One, now Ascended One,
King of Glory!
History has been changed,
The page has been turned
In heaven and on earth.

Every nation, tribe, and tongue invited—
The great invitation has been extended.

Can you hear the sound of the page turning?
Names being written in the Book of Life—
Three thousand in one day when Peter spoke.

Will it turn this day?
Will a new name be written?

Can you hear the sound of the page turning?
The soon coming King awakening our hearts;
His return is not as distant as before.
May our posture be the same as this humble handmaiden's:
"May everything you have told me come to pass" (Luke 1:38),
That His purposes in heaven will be birthed on earth again
Through us.
Holy wombs, filled with holy destiny, for the glory of the King.

Can You Hear the Sound of the Page Turning in Your Life?

It is birthing time and no longer time to sit on the nest, waiting, incubating the dreams God has put within our hearts.

The page has turned and God wants to write fresh visions for our lives that will become reality. The old dreams may remain, but there will be a new freshness upon them. It will not seem like a distant dream but a present, tangible, and obtainable reality.

Always the dreams of God are far bigger than we can ever accomplish.

If we can accomplish our dreams on our own, most likely they are not the dreams of God's heart, but simply our own ideas, as wonderful as they may sound or feel.

God's dreams require faith, walking in obedience, and dependency upon Him.

We can become sentimental about what God had shown us in previous seasons, and hold on to them like an old picture album, not wanting to let go. We want to hold on to what God has spoken to us, but He has shifted, and we are still living in the last season and this holds Him up.

When God called me to Gloucester I had a very strong prophetic word from the Lord regarding the purpose He had for bringing me to this city. He communicated very clearly to me and Tom (my former husband who is now with the Lord), and we had some of the words He spoke created into a calligraphy format and framed.

We intentionally hung these framed words on a wall in the dining room. Often I would stand before these words and pray and decree them out loud as I held on to the vision, believing for it to come forth.

For years this word kept us through many battles and challenges.

After Tom died, I wondered—
Will the word continue or is the season over?

I had to process again and again. Some people said to me that there was still more to do here in this home that was used for ministry for many years, but I had to hear clearly in this now season of God.

Finally, I knew in my heart, and with some confirmations from others that the season was indeed over. God had turned the page and I needed to turn it with Him and let Him start something totally new and fresh.

We had not accomplished all that He sent us there for, but much of the vision was, and this assignment had now come to an end.

I could have held on and tried to make it happen, but I would have delayed or missed His plans for the next season of my life and I did not want to hold God up.

After living in my home for thirty years, the Lord led me to a location that was very different from the "sanctuary by the sea" my former home had become. I left behind beautiful ocean views, peaceful gardens, and the privacy of my first home. This became a three-year season of heart searching—old ways needing to be set aside and new beginnings embraced.

I moved to a lovely apartment in a unique and diverse community. It was a place of intensity in the spirit realm, and I would need to establish a place of rest for me there. It was His plan and purpose for that season. Light must be in the darkness, truth must be in the midst of deception, life must be loosed where it seems only hopelessness and despair exist.

It required me to press more into peace Himself, to be able to live in an atmosphere of anything but peace. I had to learn how to have peace rule my life within and without so I could then release it to those around me.

It was another journey and adventure into the depths of God and His very nature being formed and shaped within me in a greater capacity.

The journey continued as I sought for a home to purchase and kept hearing, "It is where I set My gaze. You will know." Months of searching had turned into years, but He kept His promise.

Donna Milham

Now I am living in a neighborhood where every yard flows into the next, and each home is in very close proximity to each other. It is more of a downtown city neighborhood with great neighbors and many opportunities to share His love!

Releasing His sound brought a gift from God into my life—a new husband who heard my ministry team and friends releasing the sound of His love at the gateway of this city. He heard the sound while working at his apartment and came to see where it was coming from. That is another story of its own, but the fruit of obedience to give Him the desires of His heart brought His gift into my life, and He gave me the desire of mine.

There is a joy and excitement that this is where God has placed me. It has been a nine-year journey to move from my first home to where I find myself in this season.

I heard the page turn for each move, and I chose to step into the unknown of what was waiting for me to discover and explore. His hand turned the page, and His hand is writing each chapter as I surrender each day to His plans and His ideas.

Emmaus Road—Can You Hear the Sound of Hearts Burning within Us?

Luke 24:13-32

The page had turned;
He was no longer physically with them,
Speaking into their lives face to face,
Eating meals with them, praying for them and with them,
Teaching them and touching others' lives with them.
The page was turned, He was gone,
The way they thought it would be was now forever changed.
He was going to write afresh on their hearts and lives.
He was going to communicate with them in fresh new ways,
And they had to let go of the previous season
And step into this now season
Or they would hold up His kingdom plans
For their lives and those around them.
They could not sit and cry and say,
"Why did this have to happen this way?
Could You not have just remained a little longer? We were not ready."
They would never have been ready.
Heaven's plans were released on earth
And they needed to align their lives with them,
And so it is with us.
It is holy alignment time—
Aligning our lives with the Father's plans for our lives
To feel our hearts burn within us.

Donna Milham

The Sound of Ten Healed of Leprosy

Luke 17:11-19

Jesus' footsteps—releasing a sound, a declaration—
He is coming, approaching; the earth knows who He is, creation knows—
Men and women whose hearts are postured in humility
To hear, see, and know.
Jesus, the messenger of the good news of the kingdom of God,
Is at hand now and
He enters a village—no name is given—and there are ten lepers—
No names are given.
Unannounced He shows up, a suddenly—
Walking naturally, supernatural as an ambassador of the Father's heart.
He enters this village and there
Standing at a distance were ten lepers
"They shouted to him, Mighty Lord, our wonderful Master! Won't you
have mercy on us and heal us?" (Luke 17:13).
I wonder—was a report of who He was brought from other places that
He had been teaching and touching lives?
Did others begin to say Jesus the healer is here?
It does not say how they knew who He was, but they called out to Him.
He responds to the sincere cry of faith—have mercy on us!
The One who came to display mercy, who is mercy,
Would not turn a deaf ear to their pleas.
These were outcasts in their village;
The only ones they had were each other—
The untouchables—ever longing to be embraced, to be included,
To be a part of was screaming from within their souls.
Jesus simply looks at them and says,
"Go to be examined by the Jewish priests" (Luke 17:14).
He does not say you are healed; no other promise was declared.
Amazingly, they obeyed—and as they went their leprosy disappeared.
If they stayed they would not have been healed,
For it takes obedience and faith to the word of the Lord

For it to be accomplished in our lives.
They did not respond to Jesus telling them
To go be examined with questions:
"What good will that do?
Everyone knows we are lepers—anyone can see that—
And we already bear the pain and shame of this,
As well as the isolation and rejection that accompanies it.
Why bother? We are too tired to go; this does not make any sense—why?"

They respond to the Master's words with hope,
For they did not cry out to any man but to Jesus the Master.
Their words touched His mercy heart, and
Father in heaven saw and heard their recognition of His Son.
They declared who He was,
Caused an alignment in the Spirit, and created a realm
Where anything was possible.
Mercy hears the cry of every heart and is moved
With compassion and action.

Only one leper, however, when he saw he was healed, returned,
Giving praise, thanksgiving, and glory to God.

This man had been suffering hopelessly,
Waiting to die a slow, excruciating death—
Each limb disintegrating.
Now sees his flesh restored, fingers growing back, toes, noses.
Picture this creative miracle happening
As he watches himself and his nine friends
Encountering heaven's creative realm.
Hear the sound of the page turning—his life will never be the same.
Scribbled on a previous page of his life—
Hopeless, rejected, despised, dying—
A new blank page with unlimited potential is opened.
He is no longer a recluse but one who is now accepted and embraced.
He can work and fit into society, hug his friends and family,

Touch and be touched—
Things we can take too easily for granted in our own lives.

The page has been turned by the mercy hand of God—
The miraculous creative words of Jesus and the leper's blind faith to obey.
"Go to be examined by the Jewish priests" (Luke 17:14)
Hung in the air as they walked that path.
They walked under and in a declaration—
A creative word from heaven.
Jesus only did and said what He saw Father doing and saying.
They walked under the healing word, and in it,
And saw the raw creative power of God.
The word didn't even have "healing" in it or anything similar to that.
They could have said, "Ridiculous—just speak healing words to us.
Where is the next one to pray for us who really knows how to pray?"
But the desperation within them caused them to respond in faith.

He returns shouting praises to God.
He didn't quietly return and thank Jesus—no, he shouts.
Even the rocks will cry out if we are silent.
Heaven hears, creation hears, the village heard him
Specifically thanking God for His healing touch.
No questions of who and what—no mixture—it was pure God.

Then he falls face down on the ground at Jesus' feet, thanking Him.
The posture of humility and thanksgiving at His eternal feet—
Soon to be pierced for you and for me
So that we would walk as He walked.
He did not fall face down at some deity or statue—no—
But at the Master Jesus' feet.
He returned to give glory to God, the One True God of mercy and hope!

Jesus addresses this—
"So where are the other nine?" Jesus asked.
"Weren't there ten who were healed?" (Luke 17:17).

He sent the healing word—confident, knowing all ten would be healed.
Though He never used the word "healing" before this in this context,
Now He is using it, stating His intent and purpose, healing all ten!

I turned the page of ten lives but only one has returned—
Only one has come to shout, praise, fall on his face, and worship.

"They all refused to return to give thanks and give glory to God
Except you, a foreigner from Samaria" (Luke 17:18).
May we not be silent but share freely,
Boldly of God's daily touches on and in our lives.
May we believe all of His words spoken to us
And hold on to the substance of the kingdom of God
Resident within each word,
For they are rich and dripping with all of heaven's attributes.

"Then Jesus said to the healed man lying at his feet,
'Arise and go. It was your faith that brought you
Salvation and healing'" (Luke17:19).

Jesus has turned the page—forever this man's life is changed.
A new chapter, a new story, a new body,
A new heart filled with future and hope.
Hopelessness has been displaced along with his leprosy.

Our spirits, souls, minds, and hearts can be leprous.
We stand apart—the enemy trying to convince us we are untouchable,
Not loved, no future or hope;
The dreams are gone, the marriage is dead, the disease is terminal,
We will never fit in or find our tribe—on and on it goes.
If we buy the lie, our hearts can become leprous, diseased,
And this will impact all of our being.
Jesus the Master steps onto the scene of our lives, and His mercy heart
hears our cries,
He longs to turn the page.

Would we obey, "Go to be examined by the Jewish priests"?
Or would we jump to another prayer line,
Refuse to follow what He was asking us to do?
What would be our response to a word
That may seem counterproductive and foolish to us?
Move here, go there, quit your job, relocate, sell your house, buy a house,
Get a new job, rent a new facility for ministry,
Don't get the surgery, get the surgery—whatever it is He says.
To hear, to obey and not question is to walk in humble and obedient faith.

He wants to speak to us afresh and anew;
He desires that our hearts would burn within us when He speaks.
It may not be with thunder and lightning,
But truth and love will cause our hearts to burn.

Perhaps we have heard Him in a particular way for years or months and
now things seem silent, Perhaps He is asking you, me, us
To listen in fresh ways.

He wants to touch any place in our hearts and lives
That has become leprous and diseased.
He wants our hearts to be whole and looking like His—
A pure and holy heart of love—
And to live our lives from and with this love.

We may have both legs and all fingers and toes,
But if we are not walking in His divine plans
Then we may have a leprous walk—
A walk that is not whole, a walk that needs His touch,
A walk that says, "Lead me on the path of life—
Teach me how to journey with Jesus the Master.

My heart burns within me as I walk with Him;
He speaks to me in many ways,
And I desire to walk with Him all the days of my life.

Can You Hear Me Now?

I am on a holy quest for silence within, allowing me the ability to hear a pin drop within my spirit. Noise pollution surrounds us in our daily lives' activities, bringing with it many distractions to our soul realm (mind, will, emotions). Can you hear the sound of the busy churning of our mental wheels, striving and struggling to figure it all out? There is a subtle sound of grating in our spirit man, competing for the *Lordship* of our day, even our very lives.

We want to run to a quiet place, to escape the endless atmospheric disturbances surrounding us. We dream of mountain cabin retreats and seashore walks. While these are needed escapes and respites, our true quest must be to learn to be still inside—this quiet within amidst the busy, noisy places of our daily journey. It is my heart's cry to live in the revelation of knowing the One who is the chief mountain. This was the journey of the Celtic believers—to truly know the One who created all of the mountains—and as they sat in quiet contemplation in their native highlands they would fellowship with this Mountain Maker, their Rock, their Shelter, their Fortress. They sat in awe of the Creator who longs to commune with His people, and He is inviting us to discover and live what they and others have discovered.

This silence leads us to 1 Thessalonians 1:5: "For our gospel came to you not merely in the form of words but in mighty power infused with the Holy Spirit and deep conviction."

This word "power" is our word for dynamite. It is the Fourth of July within, explosive with colors and sounds of the Creator's power releasing the awe of His holy wonders. The church cries out for power, but often we can lack the foundation from which it is received—communion with the One who is all power and who gives to us His power for His purposes.

We are to be a people settled inside, pioneering outwardly, surefooted and steadfast in our gait. Because of our silence, we are able to hear the slightest whisper of a change of direction or plans from above.

There is no lack of "cell towers" for the purpose of receptivity, for Holy Spirit is within. The only time of disconnection is if we choose to tune out His voice. The Father is always speaking. The question is, are we listening?

Are our batteries charged daily in His Word and presence? Is "home" on speed dial? "Ask me and I will tell you remarkable secrets you do not know about things to come" (Jeremiah 33:3 NLT). There is no need for roaming features or charges—we have direct access 24/7/365.

Some say God is a gentleman. I agree to a point. I also believe in His holy jealousy. I believe He is rudely interrupting our lives in this hour. He is breaking into unholy conversations with the Enemy of our lives and disconnecting dialogue of discontentment with unhealthy soul friends. The question is—do we redial, frantic and frustrated when He disconnects? Or do we understand His call to silence within? How silent is this? Silent enough to hear a pin drop!

God is after every interruption between Himself and us, even those things we call good. The world doesn't seem to be able to exist very long without its cell phones—there is a restlessness of constant communication. Could it be that this somehow makes us feel value, worth? Our phones ring and we are not alone anymore. How many minutes in a week or month do we spend in conversation with others; 100, 200, 600, 1,000 minutes? How many minutes do we spend dialoguing with Him? Something to ponder!

"My heart has heard you say, 'Come and talk with Me.' And my heart responds, 'Lord, I am coming'" (Psalms 27:8 NLT).

Holy dialogue with a holy God, in this we receive divine revelation of Him—He in us, us in Him. Slowly our speed-dial numbers are used less and less and we respond to His invitation of Psalm 27.

"Why," you ask, "is this important?" To be able to hear a pin drop? Because it means there is clarity of communication—no interference, no static, no crossed lines.

We, His people, are to walk and live in truth and lead others to the truth—the person of Jesus Christ. We must hear Him clearly to be able to convey with clarity His message of restoration to a world living in the static of communication from the dark pit below. This unholy static disrupts destinies and leads many astray to dead-end paths, false hopes and dreams, confusion, and bewilderment.

Telemarketers from Satan's communication headquarters dial into our minds and souls. We have built in delete buttons from the Word of God: "We capture, like prisoners of war, every thought and insist that it bow in obedience to the Anointed One" (2 Corinthians 10:5).

When the phone of our soul rings with "out of area," why do we even answer?

When the Father calls, it reads, "Home"!

The frightening part is we can be too busy, tired, distracted to answer Him when He calls. He sometimes, out of His pursuing love, causes us to "be still" through circumstances He allows. We cry out and kick in our restlessness and lack of activity, but He holds us close; He pins us down with His arm of love and says,

"Shh!"

Will we give way? Will we give in?

"Can you hear Me now?" says the Lord.

Chapter Two: The Sound of Resurrection

The Sound of Weeping at His Feet

John 11

Mary was weeping at His feet for her brother Lazarus who had died,
Weeping for this great loss in her life.
Do we weep at His feet for a resurrection
Of our lost dreams, visions, destinies, lost children?
Weeping at the feet of the resurrected King—
Will we move His heart with tenderness and compassion?
Will He then say—

> Where did you bury your dream?
> Where did your vision die?
> Where did your destiny get put?
>> In a tomb of hopelessness and despair?

Will we hear Him say, "Roll away the stone" (John 11:39)?
> Dreams, come out of the tomb!
> Visions, return!
> Destinies, be unwrapped and loosed upon them again!

"'Martha,' Jesus said, 'you don't have to wait until then.
I am the Resurrection, and I am Life Eternal.
Anyone who clings to Me in faith, even though he dies,
Will live forever. And the one who lives by believing in Me will never die.
Do you believe this?'" (John 11:25).
Weeping at His Feet, we cling for the lost dreams of others—
Will we move His heart to tears?
"Then tears streamed down Jesus' face" (John 11:35).
Will we hear Him say, "Roll away the stone"?
Will we rise from His feet of intimacy and prayer and stand before
The tombs of hopelessness and despair, of forgotten and lost dreams,

Of sickness and disease and cry out,
        "Roll away the stone"?
Will we be His voice releasing His resurrection power and authority?
Will we remove the grave clothes and speak life, life, life—
Resurrection life?
Dare to dream again,
Dare to write the vision again,
Dare to walk out your destiny.
Impossible dreams become reality,
Resurrection truth,
        Resurrection reality.
The dead rise,
        Dead dreams rebirth,
            Destinies fulfilled
At His feet—miraculous signs and wonders come forth.

Donna Milham

Can You Hear the Sound of the Stone Being Rolled Away?

Resurrection stone,
Angels descended,
Holy light—heaven's strength rolled away the stone
They thought would hold Him,
But what could hold it back?
What decree or signet ring's seal
Of the earthly realm
Could hold back
Eternity's promise
Of the risen, resurrected King?
The Lamb who is now the Lion
Who is the Lamb—
Death, hell, and the grave
Swallowed up in the
Eternal One's roar.
I AM alive forevermore!

Can you hear the sound
Of the stone being rolled away?
Of revelation—
Hearts and minds captured
In unbelief,
Watered down doctrines,
Locking us into religion's system
Of powerless Christianity?
Yes, the angels have
Descended again,
Freeing minds and hearts
From tombs of knowledge
Without power,
And a radiant, glorious,
Power-filled church

Can You Hear the Sound?

Is coming out of the
Tomb of dead works
And philosophical debates!
He will again
Turn the world upside down.

The sound of the stone being rolled
In their ear gate—
He is risen!
Go now and preach the kingdom of God;
Set each one free
From captivity!
Holy love's release,
Rolled away stone,
Still echoes across the galaxies
Who can stop it?
What can stop it?
Graves—tombs of hearts,
Minds, souls
Rolled away—
Releasing resurrection power
To its captives.
Hear the weight of the stone
Rolling,
Each scraping sound a decree
Of freedom.
The tombs of dead religion
Being emptied
At heaven's command,
At creation's groan.
Where are the sons of the day?
Where are the sons of light?
Where are the sons of resurrection glory?
Here they come
And see the fire in their eyes.
Freedom's fire—freedom's cry!

Donna Milham

Sounds of Resurrection

Sounds of resurrection,
Waves of life,
Waters of life,
Shepherd's flute,
Rhythm of life—
Songs of those gone before you.
Risen resurrected one
Singing with heavenly choirs—
Songs of life.
Heaven and earth meeting,
Heaven's colors released—
Fuchsia, heart of flesh;
Green, new life.
Dead and broken hearts being made alive,
Waters of resurrection life,
Shepherd's flute calling,
Arise, arise!
Beat, beat with life!
Arise, arise,
Live, live, live,
Life, life, life,
Resurrection life!

Awaken the Dawn with the Song of Resurrection Life

Awaken the dawn with the song of resurrection life and light!
Release the sound of the bells of resurrection.
Release the sound that shakes the earth—the bells are within.
The cry of forgiveness, the cry of freedom,
The cry of deliverance,
The cry of life!
Release the bells within you and around you, calling to the nations,
Calling to America, calling to the lost.
Release the sound—this is what is within you—
when you walk in victory;
It is the sound of the overcomer—
The bells of resurrection.
The Enemy hates this sound;
He wants you to sit down and not move—anything but rise.
Resound with the sound of resurrection,
Dawn awakeners, awakening the dawn
With the song of resurrection's hope
To a hopeless world.

Donna Milham

The Sound of Stones Being Rolled Away

Destiny released.
Resurrection light, resurrection life
Resurrected One—within—being released.
Let Him out, let Him out,
Let Him out!
Awaken the dawn with a song of light and life!
Release resurrection light,
Feel the breeze, feel the wind
Across your face.
Holy wind's release
Refreshing, surrounding,
Calling you ever closer and deeper into holy obedience,
Casting off every fear and care,
No time to be unequally yoked with unbelief and fear.
Yoked only to Him,
The One who stepped out of heaven—left behind His kingly robe,
Stepped into a woman's womb
As holy seed,
Came forth as a man
To walk, to live, to die, and to rise again—
Firstborn Son of God.
Race never seen before,
You are of this race,
Purchased by His blood.
Blueprint written, penned in His blood—
Not erasable, nor changeable
But the eternal pulse of heaven.
Hear His heartbeat and heaven's rhythm;
Walk in this rhythm,
Not the rhythm of this world.
We must choose which rhythm we walk in.

Can You Hear the Sound?

It is of one kingdom—light or darkness.
Out of sync, out of step,
Cannot breathe right,
Cannot hear right,
All about the heart.
He wants to stake claim to the land of our hearts with
Divine ownership.
All of it, all of us—
No more little parcels and pieces at a time.
Sold out signs on our hearts.
Nothing left here—all is His.

Donna Milham

The Sound of Resurrection's Release

Can you hear the pawing of the horses' hooves in the heavens?
Church, come forth!
Can you hear the sound of stones being rolled away?
Church, come forth!
Bodies, minds, souls, destinies entombed,
Places of captivity within.
Holy release through His display of resurrection power;
Fourth of July has nothing on this grand display of *dunamis* light and
sound!
No fireworks can compare.
Oohs and ahhhs at man's creative display of color and light
Are overtaken by cries and shouts of those
Who are suddenly awakened within.
Stones rolled away,
Resurrected One and His light burst forth,
Blinding the enemy and his lies.
Holy light bearers
March across the earth again,
Crying, decreeing:
Let there be light!
Can you see it, America,
As we tread upon the enemy with light and life
In holy peace—in rhythm with the Lion and the Lamb,
The Son arising, dawn awakeners,
Stepping into the night?
His light illuminating,
We are torches—holy lights.
He thrusts us into the night—into the darkness of lives and this nation—
And darkness rolls back like a canopy
As light overtakes.
When we open our mouths, roars of light release governmental authority,
The king-priest anointing,
The roar of His jealous love,

The roar of His authority, jealousy, justice.
Where is the sound of the keys of His kingdom?
Unlocking, releasing,
Hear the sound of chains dropping off
Where are the sounds of justice,
The holy gavel of heaven?
Where are the cries of passion and compassion that will move
His mighty right hand to strike the gavel of heaven's justice,
Releasing its decree to earth's realm?
Where is the sound of His blood flowing
That releases mercy's cry?
Forgiven!

Can You Hear the Sound of His Blood Still Dripping?

What did it sound like?
Holy drops, dripping on Golgotha
At Calvary's cross
When His blood hit the ground.
It sounded like a life laid down by the Lamb of God,
A life laid down in holy love.
The sound of His blood
Hitting the ground released earthquakes,
Holy rumblings
Shaking the very earth's core;
The sound of sacrifice,
Holy sacrificial laid down life,
Crucified Lamb of God
Jesus! Jesus!
The sound of His blood is resurrection power.
Healing, salvation,
There is a sound.
Do you hear it?
Martyr's blood
Crying to our generation;
Don't waste our sacrifice.
Run the race!
Arise and run the race!
Take no thought for your life!
The sound of holy blood,
Spilt in holy love for Jesus,
Crying out—martyr's blood.
Awaken, oh, sons of God,
Wake up, wake up!
Do not fear death,
Do not fear death.

Can You Hear the Sound?

It has lost its sting at Calvary;
The sound of Jesus' blood is victory.
The sound of His blood is violent,
Not just to soothe our woeful guilty hearts,
But to raise us up past ourselves
To see the lost world,
The Enemy and his destructive plans,
And release the violent sound of Calvary—
Jesus' shed blood.
It is enough
For every person, every sin, every evil;
It destroyed death, hell, and the grave
For those who run to its flow.

It is the sound of eternal life
Will you release the sound?
This sound calls out to those whose lives will be laid down,
Even as the One who calls laid down His.
Laid down lives of lovers,
Some will be martyrs.

The sound of His blood cries out
Releasing mercy and grace
To every tongue, tribe and nation,
Man, woman, and child.
It declares His authority
Over all powers and principalities,
Over every false idol and image.
He alone is the risen resurrected Lord.
The sound of His blood,
Wooing the hearts of man, woman, and child
To His very heart, to His very side,
Crying out—mercy and grace!

Can you hear the sound?

Chapter Three: The Sound of Awakeners

Sounds above and on Earth

Hear the sound of His channel marker, His holy bell
Releasing the sound—this is the way; walk, journey in it.
Way of adventurers,
Pioneers and pilgrims,
Seekers of the unknown, uncharted realms of God's heart.
Let go of false securities, of known ways, comfortable places,
Discontentment—mostly because we try to hold on to "what was"
And His hand reaching out saying take hold,
Walk with Me into the future destiny, realms, and ways of My kingdom.
For each one—unique.
But where are the charts, the maps, the guarantees?
I AM is the only guarantee;
My Word is the chart;
My Spirit is the guide;
My eye is the compass;
My light is the illuminating presence—
Holy highway of radical love.
Daring to explore, to go past what man, religion,
Our own self-imposed limitations would dictate or say
To hear His heart and be fine-tuned to the sounds
Being released from heaven to earth.
To align our heart and spirit with them,
Allowing them to shape, transform, and bring us
Into holy alignment and holy release.

The Sound of the Woman Bursting Forth into the Room

"In the neighborhood there was an immoral woman of the streets, known to all to be a prostitute. When she heard about Jesus being in Simon's house, she took an exquisite flask made from alabaster, filled it with the most expensive perfume, went right into the home of the Jewish religious leader, and knelt at the feet of Jesus in front of all the guests. Broken and weeping, she covered his feet with the tears that fell from her face. She kept crying and drying his feet with her long hair. Over and over she kissed Jesus' feet. Then she opened her flask and anointed his feet with her costly perfume as an act of worship" (Luke 7:37-38).

Her bursting forth into the room uncovered and revealed within each one's hearts what was hidden deep inside—judgment, accusation.

Her heart released sounds of gratitude,

> Sounds of passion, sounds of abandonment
>
> Breaking open, pouring forth—
>
> Man's opinion didn't matter nor stop her.

May we be those whose hearts release sounds of broken, wide open hearts of holy worship flowing from adoration, hearts that have been awakened in love's embrace. Lovers who do not react to the opinions of man nor are they held back by their own fleshly fears and human limitations. Lost in the realm and sound of heaven, we seek to venture to become sojourners of the realm from which we were born again.

Donna Milham

The Sound of Dawn Awakeners

Psalms 57:8
"Awake, O my soul, with the music of His splendor-song!
Arise my soul and sing His praises!
My worship will awaken the dawn,
Greeting the daybreak with my songs of light!"

Dawn awakeners
Releasing a song and a sound of an army rising,
Awakened within, unstoppable!
Resurrection light shines upon their souls,
Awakening songs come forth.

Awakening the Night

"The LORD blanketed Egypt in darkness" (Psalms 105:28 NLT).
You who are Light awakens our soul.
We cannot of our own inept wisdom
Think we are wise enough, smart enough
To find You.
No, You draw—You woo.
You draw back the blanket of darkness over our souls and captivity
And You awaken our spirits with Your holy light of revelation.
Holy Spirit, fan the rays of truth and light into our very being,
That we might hear, see, understand, and choose.
Veils of darkness over minds—
Who will lift the veil?
Where are the sons of light?
Praying, going, releasing—holy light and truth,
So others can choose eternal life and light.

Can You Hear the Sound?

Veil lifters—arise!
Light releasers—shine!
Let there be light and life!

For all those who sit in the shadow of death,
Behold a light has come;
It is in you and me.
The babe in a manger,
Now the eternal King
Reigning.
Death has lost its sting for sons of light.
Dawn awakeners—lift the veil of darkness and night
With songs, sounds, moves, decrees of light;
Open wide your mouths and see its release.
Words of mercy, truth, and grace
Pulsing with light and life.

Donna Milham

Good Morning, Dawn

A song of awakening comes forth from our hearts, souls,
And spirits out of loving response.
It is an overflow—a moment of joyous celebration from our hearts.

A special moment, a glorious day,
      Our hearts respond and burst forth.
      Our hearts sing and declare His awakening love and light
          In our lives.

"Merciful God! Open Your grace-fountain for me" (Psalms 57:1).
Psalm 57 begins with declarations of God's nature and character—
That He is merciful.
David understands this mercy firsthand.
He is not a perfect man, but his heart is right and following hard after God;
      God Himself said that David was a man after His own heart.

Moses also understood and had encountered the One who is mercy.
"Moses responded, 'Then show me your glorious presence.'
The Lord replied, 'I will make all my goodness pass before you,
And I will call out my name, Yahweh, before you.
For I will show mercy to anyone I choose,
And I will show compassion to anyone I choose'"
(Exodus 33:18-19 NLT).

God tells Moses what His glory is—
It is His goodness, His kindness, and His mercy.
This is who God is—kind, good, merciful; He is mercy.
When we have a revelation like this in our hearts from encounter,
      We will burst forth with proclamation and
      Cry out in great joy.

David's cry is for a grace fountain.
Picture a fountain with water always flowing up and gushing out—

A never ending flow—
This is David's experience.
He is asking for God's never ending fountain of grace to open for him;
He is painting a picture with words of who God is—merciful—
> And from mercy flows a grace fountain over our lives,
> Which enables us to do and be all He created us to become.

He then says, "For You are my soul's true shelter" (Psalms 57:1).
This is the place His mind, will, and emotions
Have come to find rest and peace in—
In Him—in the shelter of His mercy and grace.
He says, "I will hide beneath the shadow of Your embrace" (Psalms 57:1).
David knows this place—His embrace—the divine embrace that never lets go. We can remove ourselves from it, but His eternal arms are ever open to us and His shadow is over us, for He is the hovering, brooding eternal One Desiring to hold us in—eternal love's embrace!

"He will send a Father's help from heaven to save me" (Psalm 57:3).
Not maybe or perhaps. He will send a Father's help—
The One who will always be there,
> Trusted, faithful, the ever watching Father's help
> Eternal help from above.

"My heart, O God, is quiet and confident" (Psalms 57:7).
David's declaration before His God—songs that say
This is the condition of my soul and my heart.

"Now I can sing with passion Your wonderful praises!" (Psalms 57:7).
Why? Because again and again God reveals who He is to David
In the midst of trouble, trials, and injustice.
> David's response is to sing a psalm,
> So he begins to sing with passion his praises from his whole being.

"Awake, O my soul, with the music of His splendor-song" (Psalms 57:8).
We should not look at the Enemy's schemes of destruction

And align our souls with those plans.
No, we need to be awake and sing out loud the splendors of God—
    This One who is pure and shining and brilliant.
So David sings over himself to awake;
He does not wait for another or for a corporate worship gathering—
He sings to himself.

"Arise my soul and sing His praises!" (Psalms 57:8).
Arise—stand up, do not stop, do not live in fear,
Do not let the Enemy influence you to shrink back or sit down.
No, arise and sing His praises—
Not songs of defeat, doom, gloom, sad songs of yesterdays—
Sing His praises—
Who He is, what He has done, is doing, and will do.
    For He never changes—
    Sing confidently His praises!

"My worship will awaken the dawn" (Psalms 57:8).
It is David's personal choice, decision,
And declaration that his worship will awaken the dawn.
He knows who he is and the power of a song
That springs forth from his heart and spirit—
That it will cause the dawn to awaken.
    Creation will respond, creatures will respond—
    True light always illuminates and awakens.

"Greeting the daybreak with my songs of light!" (Psalms 57:8).
He sends out a decree, greeting daybreak; dawn awakens.
Now daybreak is here—his personal songs of light greet daybreak.
It is a holy collision—a holy greeting—good morning, dawn!
I am a son of light; I release His light—this Holy One.
I release His song of light from within me.
Daybreak responds;
    Brilliant sun illuminates the earth
    Warming the soil and men's hearts—it is a new day.

"Wherever I go I will thank You. Among all the nations they will hear my
praise songs to You" (Psalm 57:9).
He will sing his songs anywhere, everywhere, songs of praise of what?
"Your love is so extravagant" (Psalm 57:10).
This is from encounter, reality—he bursts forth; he cannot hold it back.
Can you hear it—exuberant, lavish songs of boasting of His love?
Describing it so all can understand God's love is extravagant.

"It reaches to the heavens! Your faithfulness so astonishing,
It stretches to the sky!" (Psalm 57:10).
What can reach to the heavens from earth or stretch to the sky?
Nothing in the natural I can think of. His love is like no other,
And His faithfulness is beyond what words can describe.
When we talk of His faithfulness, are others astonished? Are we?
So now David is beside himself as he goes deeper and higher—
As he unfolds this song
I can see him throw his head back
And can hear his resounding voice releasing:

"Lord God, be exalted as You soar throughout the heavens.
May Your shining glory be shown in the skies!
Let it be seen high above all the earth!" (Psalms 57:11).
For all to see—not just me—
I want all to see Your shining glory, for Your name to be exalted.

The world is waiting to hear and see—will we declare, will we decree,
Will we sing out loud with no apologies from our encounters with God?
Encounter—we hear the still small voice of God as we read His Word and
Suddenly the written Word becomes alive and
We see what we have never seen before.
        We are undone.
It is taking a walk and suddenly the beauty of His creation
Causes our hearts to be quickened with

His magnificence in all of His handiworks and
      We bow low.
Encountering Him and His Word and seeing His face—
Oh, Lord, give us an insatiable hunger for You
And daily encounters with You.

Encounter—Songs of Awakening— Songs of Light

Luke 1, Mary's song of praise—her heart's response from encounter.
An angel appears and declares that Holy Spirit will—
Not maybe, but will—come upon her.

This is the third person of the Trinity—
The One who did all that the Father and Son spoke into existence.
This third person of the Holy Three is about to descend upon Mary,
And her life will be forever changed.

Encounter—the power of God Himself—
The seed of Father will be implanted in her womb.
This is beyond anyone's imagination; this is the holy realms of heaven.
The One who said light, stars, and moon and they were—
This God who actually sang creation into being
Now sends His eternal plan through Gabriel—
Messenger angel who is around the throne, up close with God.
This power that can create or destroy galaxies with one look—
One word
Will now overshadow her!
How do you prepare for such an encounter?
You don't go to your favorite boutique
And buy a dress or book a hair appointment;
You don't text your friends, send an e-mail, or put it on your webpage.

Mary is in the middle of an encounter with an angel from God's presence;
He unfolds the rest of the message ending with
"Not one promise from God is empty of power,
For with God there is no such thing as impossibility!" (Luke 1:37).
She understands that she must accept this declaration into her heart.
There it will swallow up any fear or doubt
And will make room

Donna Milham

Only for this spoken Word and Promise to be implanted.
She responds, "This is amazing!
I will be a mother for the Lord!" (Luke 1:38).
Her response of surrender to an encounter of heaven—
"I accept whatever he has for me.
May everything you have told me come to pass" (Luke 1:38).

This is now written on the tablet of her heart.
She has been told of Elizabeth becoming pregnant
And what people were saying—
And she goes to visit her after a few days.
I believe she waited a few days because her encounter overtook her—
Light, heaven's atmosphere, the radiance of Gabriel
From the throne room of God,
Declarations of light and Holy Spirit coming up close.
She didn't just get up and go back to normal life;
She has had a life changing encounter—
All of her dreams in a moment are set aside
        Gladly, willingly for His.
How does one do this—lay it all down?
Encounter.
You may not have an angel visit, but His love and spoken words to you
Cause you to respond the same as Mary.

She waits a few days
and I believe she is pondering, thanking, singing, praying,
Humbled, quickened, awestruck, stunned—
What will this be like?
There is no book to read—no one who has experienced this before.
Who would believe her? Who will understand?
"I know! Elizabeth will! For she has had an encounter with
The impossible to possible realm of God and heaven!"

Elizabeth's spirit was awakened at the sound of Mary's greeting to her, and
She began to declare over Mary and the seed in her womb.

Can You Hear the Sound?

This released Mary's song of praise to burst forth—
It was not rehearsed but burst forth.
For days she had meditated and pondered all that had taken place and
Now, like a fountain or gushing river,
She sings out loud her beautiful response—
She sings of His mercy and His faithfulness and His promises.

There it is again—declarations of who He is and His nature:
Mercy, compassion, kindness.
From Genesis to Revelation that thread of who God is
When encountered releases songs of awakening and songs of light!

She sings of His promises of mercy
From one generation to the next generation—
His promise is forever.
She stayed with Elizabeth three months—
What did those three months look like?
I believe many leapings of the babies in their wombs as
Holy Spirit would come again and again and again.
I believe songs, dances, decrees, prayers, tears of joy,
Awe and wonder, and sharing of how their lives will never be the same—
Costly responses, Accusations from eyes blinded unable to see
Divine possibilities.
Would we see, if it were today?
Do we see?

The Bible never tells us what it looked like
When Holy Spirit came to her—
Holy, intimate, secrets of heaven.
We know the fruit—Jesus came into the world to reveal His Father,
Show us heaven, show us who we were called to be
And how to live as sons of God—
To restore us to relationship with Father God.
Encounters—divine encounters—with love Himself—God is love.

Donna Milham

Songs of awakening, songs of light,
Sounds of colors, light, and movement.

Waiting, encountering love Himself, mercy Himself—
Let Holy Spirit hover and brood over you,
Let fountains of grace burst forth over you, and
May the response of songs of awakening and light
Come forth from within!

Chapter Four: The Sound of Personal Encounter

Can You Hear the Sound of Peace?

The sound of peace—
Jesus released the sound of peace as He walked.
Light and joy released from His face and eyes.
People were drawn to this sound of peace He released.
We are to release this sound of peace
In a world filled with noise and calamity.
Holy peace!

Where Is the Sound of His Finger Writing?

Breaking off accusation, slander, gossip, opinion, debate,
All opposite the fruit of the Spirit
Breaking off—you will never be anything, you are only a woman,
Only a poor man.
The same finger that wrote the Ten Commandments—
Finger of salvation, future, and a hope—
What is He writing about you, son or daughter of the Most High God?
Righteous, precious, Mine, redeemed, valued,
Priceless, purchased by My blood, promised bride—
Look into His eyes right now and see what He sees.
See the reflection in His eyes of how He sees you; let it transform you.

Where Is the Sound of the Holy Kiss of Heaven?

Causing one to dare to risk again,
To dare to love again.
Do you love Me enough to risk again?

Do You Hear the Sound of Birthing?

I heard it in the Spirit—do you hear the sound of birthing?
It is coming upon My people.
It is coming upon the land.
It is coming from the very desire of Father above.

The sound of waters breaking—
Those who have carried within their spiritual wombs the very purposes
and dreams of the Father's heart,
Impregnated in times of holy intimacy with the One they love—
This passionate Lover of their souls.
They said yes to carry His desires,
His longings and see them come forth in
His time and His way for His glory.
Some have carried within their wombs for many years,
Waiting, pondering, watching, listening;
The spiritual babies within are stirring;
It is getting close.
The time of birthing is upon us.
Heaven is weaving together hearts—hearts of family,
Hearts that will care for and nourish the dreams of His heart that are
Ready to be birthed upon the earth.
Heaven is gathering family
Who will love and embrace the ones whose lives will be

Donna Milham

Impacted, saved, healed, delivered and will
Need a people, a family, a home to be part of.
Can you hear the sound of celebration?
Sons and daughters, fathers and mothers, family—
All invited to His great love feast,
Eating at the Father's table together with holy joy.
Feasting on the very substance of who He is—
Love, joy, peace, mercy, grace, truth—
He speaks into their hearts and they awaken with destiny to be like Him,
To love like Him, to be ambassadors of His kingdom of love—as family.

Womb of the Dawn

Psalms 110:3

Womb of birthing,
Sons of light,
Sons of holy light,
There is no darkness within them.
Radiating luminaries,
Filled, oozing beams of light and life,
Sounds of waters—not the Red Sea parting,
But of waters bursting—breaking open and bringing forth sons
Of the kingdom of light
That will overtake and push back the darkness.
They have given themselves freely,
These ones who will birth sons of the dawn and sons of light.
In their mouths will be arise, arise, arise and shine!
The hour is at hand to arise and to shine!
It is not tomorrow but this very day.
Light will come forth from their mouths
And overtake dark lies and veils and
Consume with the holy presence of the Radiant One within.
Pulsating, throbbing light of mercy and grace,
Like a lighthouse on a steep cliff or craggy shoreline that sends forth
Life signals:
This is the way—walk ye in it;
Once you were darkness, now you are light;
Walk as children of light.
Holy, holy, holy, holy, holy!
By grace, by surrender,
Willingly volunteering, enabled by His empowering and might,
Light of resurrection power—this is not a little light.
It is *dunamis*—explosive—blinding to the enemy,
Awakening to the bride, calling to the prodigal, and a beacon to the lost.
Hear the sounds of waters breaking—birthing—sons of the dawn.

Donna Milham

Bright Morning Star is rising with healing in His wings;
No more shadow lands.
Gray, overtaken by light within and without.
What can stop holy declarations of life and light?
They rush across the sea like a mighty wind,
Carrying the power of the One who is all brilliant and bright;
Speed of light—flashes of truth go forth,
Splitting apart in a moment
What man's wisdom could never accomplish,
Demolishing strongholds and lies.
There is a sound, a sound, a sound of dawn's womb.
Birthing awakeners
Awaken the dawn with a song,
Awaken the dawn with a song.
They move and release light,
Dance of light and life,
Twirling and swirling, light flashes from hands and feet and eyes,
Drummers' sticks and hands releasing lightning of authority,
Demolishing schemes, plans, strategies of darkness,
Crushing them with revelatory rhythms of light—
Kingdom light and authority.
Words of teachers come forth suspended in the air—
Pulsing with deliverance, wisdom, and understanding—
Opening minds, depositing heavenly virtue and revelation.
Painters' canvases alive—no flat colors—
Alive with reflection of heavenly realms seen now on earth,
Not from the soul but from visitation and presence.
Holy light's presence is standing, watching, waiting;
Heavenly beings in battle array watching, waiting
To be released by sons of light.
Arising, awakening,
Running forward into the night
In holy light, with holy light,
He thrusts them into the darkness and through us declares,
"Let there be light!"

The Sound of Women Being Set Free

Hear the sound of My women
Ripping off labels put on by spirits of religion and doctrines of man.
Taking off garments
They were never meant to wear, not made in heaven,
Not suited for His bride-to-be!
Hear the sound of ripping off of
Lies, deception, religion, rejection, isolation, limitation, unworthiness,
No value, no place, tolerated, Jezebel.
"Remove the chains of slavery from your neck,
O captive daughter of Zion" (Isaiah 52:2 NLT).

The Sound of Women Arising

Up and out of the graves and caves of obscurity
Into His resurrection light,
Fully alive,
Fully adorned,
Fully endorsed,
Fully empowered,
By the Lion, who is the Lamb, who is the Lion—
Lionesses, dens of holy light and love,
Eyes ablaze, hearts ablaze from intimacy with His heart and His eyes.
Sound of women (sons) of God,
Opening their mouths with His breath and His roar.

Chapter Five: The Sound Of Belonging and Sonship

Can You Hear the Sound of Authority?

The Lord spoke a word to me on April 20, 2007:
> "Not all will go to Israel and touch the Western Wall, but all can come into My heart and lean against and touch the walls of My heart and be moved by My passions and emotions."

"One day Jesus said to His disciples, 'Let's get in a boat and go across to the other side of the lake.' So they set sail. Soon Jesus fell asleep. The wind rose, and the fierce wind became a violent squall that threatened to swamp their boat. So the disciples woke Jesus up and said, 'Master, Master, we're sinking! Don't you care that we're going to drown?' With great authority Jesus rebuked the howling wind and surging waves, and instantly they stopped and became as smooth as glass. Then Jesus said to them, 'Why are you fearful? Have you lost your faith in me?' Shocked and shaken, they said with amazement to one another, 'Who is this man who has authority over winds and waves and they obey him?'" (Luke 8:22-25).

Do you hear the sound of faith versus fear and authority?

The waves crashing, the men screaming, Jesus sleeping—
The sound of peace and rest.

Sound of authority—what did He say? Be still, peace?

As a man not yet raised,
He received His authority in the wilderness;
He defeated it with the sound of,
"For it is written in the Scriptures" (Luke 4:4).
       He received His power in humility—

Do you hear the splash of His baptism in the Jordan with John?
He received His destiny and affirmation through obedience:
    "My Son, you are my beloved one" (Luke 3:22).
The three disciples received His identity on the mount—
    The sound of the chatter of Peter,
    The silence after the Father spoke:
"This is my Son, my Beloved One" (Luke 9:35).
    Moses and Elijah appearing,
    Holy appearing of the cloud of witnesses,
Sound of thunder will again be heard—
    One holy foot on the sea and one holy foot on the earth.
Sound of authority must be in us—this will take great humility—
    Sounds like lives crashing to the ground—
        Here I am! Send me!
    Not for my will and my name, but for Your name!
    Sounds like His holy desires and not ours,
"But one day when you are old, others will tie you up
And escort you where you would not choose to go—
And you will spread out your arms" (John 21:18).
    A life no longer your own,
Sound of Patmos—what did that lonely island of rock sound like?
        Depends on who was exiled there—
    A son of God or a slave of self and the world?
  A son of God would release praises to be considered worthy to
        Suffer for and with Him,

        To worship.

Donna Milham

The Sound of His Glad Welcome

Luke 15

Because of Christ and our faith in him, we can now
come boldly and confidently into God's presence
(Ephesians 3:12 NLT).

The Prodigal Son had begun his journey home and was not sure of the reception he would receive from his father and his brother. In the distance he heard a sound—a sound of glad welcome. His father had been watching and saw him coming and called for a ring, a slipper, his robe, and for a fatted calf to hold a feast—a celebration. This music began releasing a sound of sonship and belonging into the atmosphere that would surround his Prodigal Son.

As the son got closer he could hear it more clearly. Could his heart believe it—could this be possible? What is this sound I hear? His father runs to him; the prodigal drops to his knees and falls into his father's arms and begs his forgiveness.

The sound of sonship and belonging brings repentance. You don't have to counsel it, beg for it, demand it; it comes forth when one knows he or she is gladly welcomed and embraced; though they have fallen and blown it (not an excuse to continue in sin), they are received again.

May we release a sound of His glad welcome—calling the prodigals home into His arms.

But beware of the sound of the jealous older brother. For he also heard the music, and it stirred and released envy and jealousy; it uncovered what was in his heart all along. He was not rejected by his father. Even when the father saw and heard what was in his son's heart, he tried to console him.

His father reminded him that all that he had was his. He could have had a fatted calf and a celebration anytime—it was always there for him. All his son had to do was ask, draw near—but the son worked and worked to prove his sonship, to prove his faithfulness—yet he had never come to understand his inheritance.

As His sons, we must do the work of the kingdom, but it is from devoted love and gratitude—not to prove or earn anything. We too can be in the Father's house and not live as His heirs and sons.

Hearts that understand this revelation—people who are broken, who have lost everything, and return to the one place of hope—who are

> Embraced in glad welcome,
> Enter into the reality of a
> Future and a hope,
> And these will sing and declare and dance
> The song and dance of acceptance
> From the sound of His glad welcome.

Donna Milham

Can You Hear the Sound of His Songs of Gladness over You?

"Lord, You are my secret Hiding Place, protecting
me from these troubles, surrounding me with songs
of gladness! Your joyous shouts of rescue release my
breakthrough" (Psalms 32:7).

Can you hear the sound of His songs of gladness over you?
Songs that celebrate you that came forth from the heart of God
While He was contemplating, dreaming, and designing you.
His dream became reality—
You were suddenly a seed in your mother's womb.
You came forth—birth—on this highlighted day of eternity.
He sang His perfect song of gladness over you and over your birth,
And all of heaven joined in—it surrounded and encompassed you,
Wrapped you in a swaddling cloth
Of eternal love and celebration, and rejoiced
Over the day you were born.
A song just for you—notes danced across the sky like shooting stars,
Creation saw and heard
There is only one you—unique—never to exist again.
He delights so deeply in each and every aspect
Of His glorious design—you.
For all of your days, this song is within and around;
The circumstances of life will attempt to erase it, delete it,
But it is written—embedded on the hard drive of your very spiritual DNA.
The noise and calamity of the world's kingdom
Will attempt to drown it out,
Vying and competing to govern your soul with its hopelessness and fear,
Trying to take captive your mind, will, and emotions—your very being—
But there He is—your Creator,
Suddenly on the scene.
His joyful shouts of rescue releasing your breakthrough,

For you are His from the beginning to the end.
Forever loved and cared for,
Unshakeable confidence within,
Listen for His song of gladness again.
Hear it—for some perhaps the first time.
Remember—listen again.
It is always new,
Like mercy each morning and the dew on dawn's fields;
Hear it again—His joyous shout of rescue and release—
For He is breakthrough.
What can stand in His way?
He is the way, the truth, and the life;
This is the One—who sings, who shouts,
Who rescues, who releases—you.

Chapter Six: Can You Hear the Sound of the Father's Voice?

Mountain of Transfiguration (Mark 9:1-7)

Jesus took Peter, James, and John with Him to the top of the mountain to be alone with Him, Separated from distractions, throngs, of people and their needs.

I believe one of the reasons Jesus brought them here was to teach them the posture of waiting.

Jesus went to the mountains often to pray, to be with His Father—to wait! He knew this was the foundation they needed for their destinies to be fulfilled.

He brought them to the place of waiting, communion, and visitation where He received Revelation from His Father's heart, worshiped, adored, and met with heaven—His home.

How did He live here on earth—as a man, once God?

I believe He lived in, and within, intimate heart communion with His Father and Holy Spirit.

He was not of this world, but here to fulfill His Father's desire, to restore His children to Him and receive the promise of His bride.

He brings Peter, James, and John to this place—His place—the top of the mountain where

No one else is—where no one else can see or hear the divine exchange of their hearts.

The waiting place.

In this place Jesus' appearance suddenly changes; His clothes also become dazzling white.

No earthly process could do this; this was heavenly transformation—heaven's touch.

When heaven touches earth, people are transformed.

Why touch heaven—why cry out for visitation—why wait?

For transformation.

Elijah and Moses suddenly appear and begin to talk with Jesus.

"Peter blurted out, 'Beautiful Teacher, this is so amazing to see the three of you together! Why don't we stay here and set up three shelters: one for you, one for Moses and one for Elijah?'" (Mark 9:5).

How did Peter know who they were? He was not alive when they were on the earth.

I believe it was the Spirit of wisdom and revelation that was upon them,

Giving them understanding and knowledge within the cloud.

Peter and the others were afraid—he spoke from the place of not knowing what to do;

He just spoke out, as we can often do, presumptuously.

He was still in need of being taught the lesson of learning to wait, watch, and be still—

To experience for himself how to wait in the holy presence of God the Father.

They stood there afraid, having just interrupted a holy conversation—a visitation.

A cloud comes over them, a voice speaks,

"This is my most dearly loved Son—always listen to him!" (Mark 9:7).

Suddenly they look and Moses and Elijah are gone; only Jesus is with them.

I believe the Lord is coming like this again—

In a cloud, into our meetings, into our homes.

He wants to overtake our meetings and gatherings with His presence.

He wants all eyes on Jesus and all ears listening to His Son.

He will visit us and He will interrupt us.

Some of us may be speaking foolishly and interrupting visitations of God,

Planning what we will build and do with it or doubting it.

But God will make it clear—

It is all about My Son; listen to Him.

Listen, wait, listen.

He brings us up the mountain to listen, to see, and be changed forever.

He wants to put within us the hope of what it will be like at the end—

In the twinkling of an eye when God's saints are caught up.

What visitation can look like, sound like, and feel like here and now—

To encounter the cloud of His presence.

Peter eventually knew what it was to walk and live within

The shadow of the cloud of His Presence over him.

I believe Jesus' whole being was radiant—He is the Radiant One, the Glorious One—

They saw Him in His resurrected state before it ever happened.

They did not know it was a seed of revelation going into their spirits

That would one day agree with what their physical eyes would see again—

Only this time Jesus dead, buried, rising again as the resurrected King of Glory and Light.

Chapter Seven: Mary's Prophetic Song and Sounds

"My soul is ecstatic, overflowing with praises to God!
My spirit bursts with joy over my life-giving God!"
(Luke 1:46).

Why—why was her soul overflowing? Why would ours overflow?
Because, "For he set his tender gaze upon me,
his lowly servant girl" (Luke 1:48).

Heaven knew who Mary was—His watchful eye ever upon her—
Her heart posture responses in everyday life in her heart toward her God.
A heart of tender, sweet adoration with humble obedience,
Who lived to bring Him joy and pleasure each and every day.

I believe Mary was a young woman who walked
To the beat of a different drummer,
That she heard the realms of heaven in her daily life.
I believe she strolled fields and streams
And worshiped from a place of simple
Yet profound adoration of the One she loved.
I believe that the Father's gaze rested upon her;
Heaven was fascinated by this young woman's heart—
Chosen by God to carry the third person of the Trinity.
The holy gaze of heaven—
Can you sense the penetrating, purposeful eyes of Father
Looking into her heart and spirit?
This womb needed to be a holy womb, holy before Him and with men.
He was not looking for a king or queen, fancy adorned garments,
Or an elaborate home—
He was looking for a heart and a womb of royal heritage from above—
One who loved God with all of their being and walked in meekness.

This was not a weak young girl.
She would need to withstand
The persecutions and accusations of being pregnant
Before being married.
She would learn to walk in His gaze
When the gazes of man were filled with question marks and unbelief.
No one could take away her visitation.
No one could cancel out her response
To heaven's pronouncement over her life.
She declares, "And from here on, everyone will know
That I have been favored and blessed,
The Mighty One has worked a mighty miracle for me;
Holy is his name!" (Luke 1:48-49).
She is decreeing and releasing the sound
Of favor and blessing over her life.
She is not ignorant of her real life journey ahead
And what others will say or think.
But she decrees and declares the sound of truth
And creates an atmosphere to walk and live in—
A cloud of a holy decree about a holy God and His promises,
Living in His gaze.
For He did not look away after Mary was impregnated with His Son—
His eye of favor and blessing was upon her and
She chose to live in the truth and reality of His gaze and His decrees.

Can you hear her song still pulsating through the galaxies?
Holy is His name.
See her radiant, joy-filled face, hear her spirit bursting with joy—
Filling the heavens with song, permeating the earth with sounds.
Holy is His name.
Gabriel had spoken to her:
"The Spirit of Holiness will fall upon you" (Luke 1:35).
She was clothed, adorned, in-filled with the Spirit of Holiness.
Supernatural realms of heaven, the atmosphere of heaven, holy—
Not a book of rules, regulations, and laws.

No—the One who is holy,
The place that is holy,
The realms that are holy.
The Holy Spirit Himself came upon her to impregnate
And impart holy realms of heaven—
The realms the Son of God, the second person of the Trinity,
Dwelt in—in heaven.
This realm was imparted into her physical womb—
He would be incubated as a holy seed,
Holy sperm from Holy Father, through Holy Spirit into a holy womb
Prepared and made ready
To host, incubate, and bring forth the Savior of mankind and the world.
These holy realms carry with them angels from on high,
Songs of adoration,
Holy hushes of awestruck wonder.

The sounds of heaven, changed—nine months—
This One is no longer in heaven but inside a virgin's womb.
Hear heaven's heartbeat inside her womb—
Do you hear the sound of eternal life—boom, boom, boom?

It says, "Almighty God will spread
his shadow of power over you in a cloud of glory!" (Luke 1:35).
She would not walk without the power of heaven
Within, around, surrounding—
She was clothed in the glory of her destiny and assignment;
For this reason she was born.
Our Father does not call us to carry dreams and plans of heaven
And then not enable, empower, enfold us into His power and glory.
Sounds and realms of holiness and the glory of heaven
Became her atmosphere,
Like a garment put upon her from above.

Can you picture that moment—
Hear the trumpets, wind, fire, angels' wings, songs, movement—

All about her heaven and earth kissed—
Divine kiss, holy kiss.

"This is why the child born to you will be holy,
And He will be called the Son of God" (Luke 1:35).
Why? Because of holy impartation and honoring—
Because a holy Father can only bear a holy Son.
Our own plans and dreams from our good ideas
Will never bring forth holy realms of heaven;
God's eye is ever looking for spiritual hearts and wombs that He can visit
And impart His holy Plans and bring them forth,
Knowing they will be stewarded and loved in the atmosphere of holiness.
An atmosphere where the reverential fear of the Lord is present,
Where the joy of salvation is always released,
Where the decrees of heaven overtake the opinions of man,
Where bowed knees, raised hands,
Surrendered hearts are ever before Him.
A people who walk in honor before Him, with Him and with each other,
Called to be a holy birthing place for heaven—
God's holy heaven to be revealed in its eternal song and sounds.
Lives are changed forevermore
And dreams of the Holy Three become tangible reality.
This requires visitation of the Holy One and time in His holy presence—
A holy kiss of the Father, the adorning of Holy Spirit,
Overshadowing presence of the Most High God.

This shadow hovered over Peter—the one who denied Jesus three times—
Would now gladly lay down his life for he no longer feared men or death,
For all of heaven was with him, in him, around him.
The shadow—the overshadowing glory—healed the sick as he passed by.
That is not just for Peter—that is our invitation also.
Do you hear the sound, the invitation—will you carry My glory?
There is a cost and not all are willing to pay the price.

I dare to say we won't without a heart of holy adoration—
The sound of holy surrender.
"May everything you have told me come to pass" (Luke 1:38).
"What's more, your aged aunt, Elizabeth,
Has also become pregnant with a son.
The 'barren one' is now in her sixth month" (Luke 1:36).

Mary had been chosen and so was Elizabeth—
The barren one who is barren no longer—
For when heaven comes down in its power
With holy decrees and purposes
Wombs are opened—spiritually and physically—
Hope becomes a reality; His suddenlies come upon us.
Immanuel—God is with us, not just a song,
But an encounter with the Everlasting One.
What would Everlasting One find this day as
He gazed upon you and me, even this very moment?
What is in our hearts for Him?
Are we living in a barren season,
A barren life with barren hearts and wombs?
Looking but not seeing the fulfillment of proclamations and promises?
Are our situations too huge, relationships too empty,
Promised dreams lost too long ago?
But a child has been given and a virgin has conceived
And Immanuel is with us.
He wants us to live in the reality of
"Not one promise from God is empty of power,
For with God there is no such thing as impossibility!" (Luke 1:37).

Promise has a sound—the sound of eternal covenant,
The sound of all of heaven and God's love backing up what He spoke.
It could be thirty years ago or thirty seconds ago,
But we must believe and enter into this experiential truth and reality.
There is no such thing as impossibility in our true home—heaven.

We must live in heaven on earth
And we must surround ourselves with those
Whose heart cry is "I believe and I receive,
For God is with me—may His will be done."
Do you believe that today?
God comes and speaks to us and we can respond,
Saying that is for him or her or them,
But God is looking for amazed hearts and glad responses.
We cannot become familiar with God—
We must be intimate with Him and respond as Mary.
"This is amazing! I will be a mother for the Lord!
As His servant, I accept whatever He has for me.
May everything you have told me come to pass" (Luke 1:38).
Holy alignment with holy decrees—
No excuses, no what ifs.
Too often we try to figure it all out before we will respond,
Or respond and then try to determine the rest—
Often many change their minds.
But God's impregnation of His Son could not be put into the womb of one
Who would change her mind.
The angel did not give her all of the details,
He declared God's purposes and plans and awaited her response.

Heaven visits and awaits our response.
I wonder, was heaven silent—hushed when it was her moment to respond?
Is heaven silent when God visits us? Awaiting our response?
Do we respond? Do we hear?

Can we hear Mary's song still hovering?
"Mercy kisses all His godly lovers" (Luke 1:50).

Abraham's willingness to sacrifice, even his son—
Barren ones, Sarah and Abraham, birth Isaac
Who was their promise and for generations to come forth from—
He offers him on the mountain of the Lord.

His "be it done unto me" moment was a lifted hand with a knife,
And in those moments
Heaven opened—
"The angel of the Lord called to him from heaven,
'Abraham! Abraham!'
'Yes,' Abraham replied. 'Here I am!'
'Don't lay a hand on the boy!' the angel said, 'Do not hurt him in any way,
For now I know that you truly fear God.
You have not withheld from me
Even your son, your only son'" (Genesis 22:9-12 NLT).
Do you hear what I hear?
Heaven's sound of provision and promise resounded and came down.
The Lord provided a ram,
And he offered the ram and Abraham named the place
"the Lord will provide" (Genesis 22:14 NLT).

From his experience he writes of what he has encountered
With the living God.
He encountered the nature of the Lord as provider—
The One who keeps His promise and makes the way and the
Provision for His promises to come forth.

Mary encounters this God and sings,
"Mercy kisses all his godly lovers,
From one generation to the next" (Luke 1:50).
Do we know the mercy kisses of God?
Do we tell our children—natural and spiritual—
And sing of His mercy kisses?
What are His mercy kisses for you?
Ponder them afresh in your hearts,
Write them down, meditate and sing of them.
Release the sound and song of mercy kisses for all to hear and enter into—
Mercy songs that flow, wave after wave,
Upon those who are in awe before Him.
Let us fall on our knees, let us hear the angels' chorus,

Let us sing of that divine and holy night
That Christ came forth from heaven to earth.
Do we hear the angels' chorus? Do we fall on our knees?
Do we walk and live in holy adoration like Mary?
"My soul is ecstatic, overflowing with praises to God!" (Luke 1:46).
God had gazed upon earth; He sought for one who would bear His Son.
He set His gaze—He looked intentionally, purposely into her heart.
One good look from above, and look what happened—
Nothing is impossible.
Not the look of a man, but God Himself.
She sang of His favor and of being fortunate.
This song would carry her through all that was ahead—
Persecution, birthing in a stable, fleeing for their lives,
The road of Calvary.
This song would hover—remember, Mary,
Mercy kisses, holy is His name, favored and blessed.
Remember, chosen one of God.
One good look—remain in His gaze!

"Those who hunger for him will always be filled" (Luke 1:53).
There is a cry in hearts of the hungry, always for more of Him;
It overtakes all other hunger and desire.
Can you hear the song of the One who was born of a virgin;
Walked the earth representing His Father in heaven;
Laid down His life on a cross for you and for me;
Rose from the dead; conquered death, hell, and the grave;
And sits at the right hand of the Father?
His song that awakens hearts and seals this with His word of eternal love:
"Place Me now as a seal of fire over your heart forevermore.
This living, consuming flame of fire will seal you
To be Mine as a prisoner of love!" (Song of Songs 8:6).

This song is the answer to Mary's question—
The question of every seeming impossibility to man,

But possible with God.
"But how could this happen? I am still a virgin" (Luke 1:34).

How could this happen?
I am too old, too young, too uneducated,
Too unnoticed, too forgotten.
The One who is fire comes upon us,
The One who is love overshadows us,
The One who is glory infills us,
The One who is life impregnates us with life from above.

"Before going home, Mary stayed with Elizabeth for about three months"
(Luke 1:56).
I believe Father wants to impart today fresh hope to hearts and spirits,
And from this place new songs will then flow from hope-filled hearts.
What He imparts
We are to wait, walk in, in the place of rest,
Let it take shape until it becomes reality within you
And your whole being aligns with hope.
It is not something you say but breathe out of your spirit—
Life and light-filled hope for the seemingly impossible
To become reality in your life.

All of us are meant to carry the glory—the One who is glory is within us.

Chapter Eight: Can You Hear the Sound of His Kingdom Authority?

Dominion's Sound

Warrior angels,
Faces brilliant light,
Glistening armor,
Swords in front of faces,
Flashing—double-edged
Swords of holy illumination
To cut through every false place
And release holy revelation,
Thrust into our very heart and being
With *let there be light*,
Piercing hearts with truth.
Be it done unto me—cry released.
Holy encounter, holy surrender—
Death to self.
Arise in resurrection attire
Of a life not your own,
Purchased costly price
Holy, holy, holy
Holy Three
Encountering
Radical resurrection army.
This army has no fear of death,
A victory key in their heart and hands.
The Enemy's armies of the end days
Give way to the sound of a resurrection army
Rising and marching forth.
Unstoppable!

The God of Glory Thunders

"Proclaim His majesty, all you mighty champions,
You sons of Almighty God! Give all the glory and strength back to Him!
Be in awe before His majesty. Be in awe before such power and might!
Come worship wonderful Yahweh arrayed in all His splendor!"
(Psalms 29:1-2).

This is our destiny and call as His sons,
Giving glory, acknowledging His strength,
Arrayed in holiness from being with Him and in Him,
Choosing our paths carefully as sons,
His name ever before us, over us, in us, around us.

The voice of the Lord is upon the waters,
Hovering over—His voice hovers and is in the waves,
Hovers over the stillness like a sea mist, like the calling of a loon;
It hovers hauntingly, calling to us in holy wooing—
Deep calling to deep.
His voice in the waves, breaking over us,
Wrapping us in holy love and holy majestic decrees.
We lie on the shores and it washes over and into our beings—
Colors of His majestic splendor.
He catches us in waves of His adoration
And speaks to our hearts of His love and might,
His voice Spirit to spirit upon waters of the deep.
For His son—no fear of His voice upon the waters.

The God of glory thunders—
His voice thunders like a giant storm, a sonic boom.
All creation responds and hears;
It shakes foundations;
It awakens hearts, souls, and spirits;
It silences; it illuminates.
It is majestic authority revealed in sound,

The voice of the Lord is majestic.
Kingly decrees—all creation bows.
Every knee will bow one day;
Elephants trumpet, lions roar, eagles soar, gazelles leap, whales breach—
The King has spoken.
All He has created responds—
Above the earth, on the earth below,
First, second, third heaven.
Shooting stars,
      Moons eclipse,
            New galaxies are formed.
Crashing waves,
      Red and purple sunsets,
            Rainbows arching.

The voice of the Lord breaks the cedars—
Strength of tall trees snap at His voice,
Strength of man independent of Him breaks in two,
Strength of kings of nations broken at His voice.
No strength apart from those who walk in holy union—holy
dependency—will remain.
He will break it, snap it, in two, three, four;
The voice of the Lord breaks in pieces the cedars of Lebanon,
So many pieces it cannot be reconstructed,
Splintered—not even good for firewood.
He shatters, splinters, demolishes places
Of independence, smugness, pride, arrogance—
There is no God, we don't need God.

All creation responds, nations respond.
He causes even nations to be out of control like a young wild ox
Or rejoice, playful like a calf.

The voice of the Lord hews out flames of fire,
All consuming fire of His enemies,

Nothing escapes.
Moves across desert plains, up mountainsides, through forests,
Laps up rivers and fields and streams,
Fills hearts of His lovers with devoted love
And holy jealousy for all that is His.

The voice of the Lord shakes the wilderness,
The places of trials and testing,
The place where the Enemy holds captive,
The desert seasons,
The places of hopelessness and despair, places of isolation
All are shaken and awakened.

Wilderness of Kadesh—
The voice of the Lord shakes the wilderness of Kadesh!
The voice of the Lord makes the deer to calf,
Causes birthing to take place.
Holy impregnations—now birthing time at the sound of His voice,
Natural and spiritual.

Strips forests bare,
So powerful the blast of His breath and voice;
Forests stripped bare—nothing is left.
All hidden things exposed,
The Enemy's strategies and secret hiding places,
Things in our hearts and lives,
No place to hide for those not His own,
All uncovered;
Earth naked, man exposed,
Every military outpost uncovered—natural and spiritual.

And in His temple everything says, "Glory!"
This glorious King,
All have seen the result of His majestic voice and respond, "Glory!"
All honor, all glory, all power to You!

It takes a people who know His voice of thunder
And walk under it and in it—
The fear-free zone—to release declarations of life
And extend His cup of life.

Donna Milham

The Sound of His Blood and His Love

Before the foundation of the earth
The One who spoke trees and fields into existence
From where the crown of thorns would be formed and shaped
And the cross made,
He provided for His own sacrifice.
Even as He provided for Abraham and Isaac
Declaring before time—I AM and always will be
The Creator, your Lover, the sacrifice, the Lamb and the Lion,
All-ruling King Eternal.
I found you and shaped you, knew you and loved you—
Then, now, and forever.
Question my love? Nevermore—get it settled once and for all.
Get the questions settled—
Every whispered doubt, every lie swallowed up
By the flow of My blood,
The flow of My blood.
Get it settled deep, deep, deep,
Eternal flow of love in My blood.
Hear it gushing and rushing toward you,
Overtaking flow into your hearts and beings,
Eternal flow of love eternal
Before the foundations.
See it, see it, see it.
Read it, read it, read it.
From Genesis to Revelation, Genesis to Revelation—
A thread of My blood's flow.
Revelation—the full release of who I AM, who I AM!
Four living creatures know and the twenty-four elders know,
Cloud of witnesses know.
Now, now, now,
Step into the now revelation of My blood and My love.

Unstoppable Ones

We are unstoppable because we have encountered the Lion of Judah,
Stood before His marvelous, majestic, mighty love
And looked into His eyes,
Fully focused,
Fully engaged,
Awestruck wonder;
And there in that moment
He opens wide His royal mouth and roars.
Fiery love shoots forth
And melts every icy place of our hearts,
Fills every timid place with courageous love,
Love that transforms us into
Unstoppable ones.
Eternal love's roar purging through our spiritual veins,
DNA,
Being,
Love like red hot lava overtaking every cell.
We don't just love;
We become love.
We are love
Because He is love.
His DNA becomes ours
In holy visitation of
His holy roar
Of holy resurrection love.
Love sent Him;
For love He laid down His life;
Love took the keys of death, hell, and the grave
And displays them in great victory and triumph.
Hear the sound of eternal victorious keys of liberty and freedom
Over you.
They sound like
Love

Donna Milham

That sets every place of captivity
Free,
Breaking open every place,
Every heart,
Every past
Invited to enter into
Future and a hope.
Eternity now is at hand—
Eternity's door.

Before us,
Living here and yet there,
Unstoppable.
We see, we hear, we know
Beyond a shadow of doubt,
Heaven's call upon our lives:
Be love,
Seek to live from another realm,
Realm of heaven
Ruled by
"For this is how much God loved the world" (John 3:16).
Not someday or one day
But today.
Today is eternity
Now and forevermore,
Eternity—eternal love,
Wrapped around us,
In us.
He clothes us in the colors and sounds of His holy creation
All revealing His love.
Wrapped in a cloak of the stars of heaven,
We illuminate darkness
With holy decrees of love like a tsunami.
Lightning bolts,
Thunder,

Can You Hear the Sound?

In the midst of morning twilight and midnight hour,
Release, release, release
Light and love,
Unstoppable.
Because love will not relent,
Heaven's mission and mandate
Will march forward,
Will dance the dominion decrees from heaven's throne:
Love won,
Love wins,
Love rules,
Mercy triumphs over judgment!
Reign in love;
Worship the One who is love.
Priests and kings of another realm,
Our true home,
Bring its truth and reality
Here, now.
No delay,
No hesitation,
Flowing into and out from
His heart to yours
To overtake.
Holy, holy, holy,
And knees bow in awe and wonder
At the Ancient of Days.
Oh, Lion, roaring over each tongue, tribe, and nation!
Hear His roar,
See where His eye is gazing and step into His
Roar and gaze:
Commission, assignment, mandate—
A life awaiting holy encounter with messengers of heaven
From another realm—
Eternal ones on assignment,
Ambassadors of love

Donna Milham

Step into His gaze.
It is the place of
Illuminating light and fire
Where His gaze is an open portal of holy revelation
And here is the open door to His heart.
Who will go and invite that one in,
That nation in,
To step into His gaze and His roar?
Eternal roar of
"You are Mine!"
To finally rest in
His divine embrace of love.

The Sound of Holy Impregnation Is upon Us

Holy impregnation time,
Who will carry Me?
Who will open to Me your spiritual womb?
Who will be inconvenienced?
Who will be willing to carry Me,
Birth Me in the hidden places?
No man knowing,
No titles or applause,
Birthing My holy purposes
In lowly manger towns
And unseen homes,
Hidden from man's eyes,
But all of heaven watches and waits and sees.
Even today
Who will open to Me
Their spiritual womb
To receive from Me?

Donna Milham

Hear His Roar of Glory

His roar releases a golden cloud of glory.
It unfolds as it comes to the earth like a garment;
In it He releases the cry of divine ownership,
A scroll calling for the laying down of our lives,
Looking for the title deeds of our hearts to be given
In divine exchange
For His scroll of divine ownership—
Mine,
Bond slaves, love slaves,
Willingly going into love's captivity within His heart,
To ever live and move and have our being in Him.
Divine visitation,
Glory cloud from His holy roar—
Unfolding,
Releasing,
Mine.

Chapter Nine: The Sound of the Eternal One

What Love Is This?

"Place me like a seal over your heart, like a seal on your arm. For love is as strong as death, and its jealousy is as enduring as the grave. Love flashes like fire, the brightest kind of flame. Many waters cannot quench love, nor can rivers drown it" (Song of Songs 8:6-7 NLT).

Love flashing like a fiery inferno—bursting forth vibrant flames;
Your jealous love—flashing, bright, intense.
Eyes can barely look because of the intensity,
But by Your grace you enable us to glance,
To even gaze at the brilliance of Your desire.

Stars in the sky—brilliant, shining, announcing, declaring
Jealous love has left heaven,
Has disrobed Himself of His divinity and has come naked,
Vulnerable onto earth as a baby, an infant crying out in holy intercession.
Man apart from God would only hear a baby's cry,
But the heavens and all of creation heard eternity's cry,
Eternal love's cry of holy intercession.
Cry and declaration—Messiah is born!
For the sake of Our holy desire and for the ones We created,
My Father and I together with Holy Spirit
I came, I have come—here I AM, here am I!
It will take eyes and hearts opened by Holy Spirit
To see who I AM,
To see I AM in a manger.
The animals knew,
They bowed and sat by, gazing at the One who spoke them into existence.
The first Adam named them,
But the last Adam has flashed upon the scene now.

Earth is poised—ready
To receive her salvation;
It groans in holy response and bows its knees.
Will mankind bow?
Will mankind see?
The shepherds, lowly in the world's eyes,
Saw and heard
Heaven's declaration
As jealous love flashed in the sky—
Pulsating, illuminating,
Declaring
Immanuel with us.
They must go—love draws, compels
Across hills and plains, on a cold wintry night;
They arise
Then must go and see what—who—heaven is announcing.
They have no gifts to offer,
They are poor and simply shepherds,
They have only the posture of bowed knees,
Of lips to declare praises,
Eyes to behold and adore.
The gift of themselves,
The gift to step away from the daily mandates of their lives
And respond to a sign in the sky.
They didn't have to go;
They could have remained on the lowly hillside.
Oh, love as strong as death,
Illuminated the sky that night.
Eyes and hearts awakened by this jealous love,
They chose to go,
Never regretting as they gazed upon
I AM,
The One who would stand in the garden.
Whom do you seek?
Jesus of Nazareth

I AM He,
And they fell at His decree.
Jealous love,
Knowing His time to drink the cup of eternal suffering and damnation,
Stood—compelled by holy desire—for a bride
He could see, smell, hold
Down the corridors of time,
And He stood in the face of hell's attempts to quench love's rescue
But this was settled.
Unshakeable love that will not stop or quit,
That presses through—that looks hell in the face and says,
"They are Mine—you cannot have them,
For the ones who will respond to My heart's desire
Will have written on their hearts and sung from their mouths—
I'm Yours!"
This will compel them through the valleys of death,
This fiery flashing fire of love
Will not be quenched.
For as they come to Me again and again,
I, the heavenly billows blow, blow, blow.
I fan the flame of holy passion and desire;
I pour in fresh oil as they come aside with Me,
Altars of hearts, flashing brilliant.
Men's eyes opened,
What is this that just passed by?
What is in the eye of this One before me?
I smell smoke,
I feel fiery heat,
Who, what is this?
It is Immanuel!
It is the Bridegroom!
It was a baby who is now the Lion-lover roaring over the earth,
"You are Mine!"

A Baby's Cry—A Lion's Roar

Luke 2:12

A baby wrapped snugly in strips of cloth—
The Lion who would roar before Lazarus's tomb,
"Roll the stone aside" (John 11:39 NLT)
And decree, come forth,
Remove his grave clothes; strips of cloth
Unraveled not at His command.
No one questioned—they obeyed.
Flesh awakened, pink again.
Blood purging, rushing, gurgling through Lazarus's veins;
Organs responding.
Heart beating in rhythm with the Lion's decree:
"Come forth!"
They unravel the strips of cloth,
Uncovering love's response to hell's grip.
Jealous love conquers death;
Hell must let go at its decrees.
Baby wrapped snugly in strips of cloth,
Can you hear the sound?
As Mary would change His strips of cloth,
Prophesying to the earth, to nations, to hell—
A day is coming
When death will lose its sting.
Hear, with each strip of cloth changing,
The prophetic decree that will be spoken at a tomb one day
And then at a cross on Golgotha's hill—
They took My robe; they could not tear it.
This robe of justice would not be torn in two.
No, for all eternity man will see the power of My robe of justice.
Torn in two—the veil separating man from Me:
Holy Three.
Ah, naked I came,

Naked I hung,
That those I love would be clothed forever
In My desire.
Hell cannot strip My bride;
I clothe her with My very look, gaze, words of love and life,
Wrap her in My decrees of beauty, passion, purity, purpose, value, worth.
I wrap her, cover her shame, sorrows, and regrets;
I AM future and hope,
I wrap her in dreams of heaven.
How beautiful are her garments,
Brilliant in color;
Did you see that flash in her heart?
Oh yes, we are one—hearts ablaze,
I am hers and she is mine.
I hung gladly,
I came willingly,
Strips of cloth folded neatly inside the garden tomb.
Rolled back stone—
Hell couldn't stop that stone from being rolled back
Nor the eternal sound it released and still releases:
He's alive forevermore!
Keys, keys, keys of life,
Conquering King,
The baby's cry is now the Lion's roar.
It was always one and the same.
Eyes to see, ears to hear, hearts to understand and respond.

Hear the Sound of the Keys of Dominion Authority

"See, my servant will prosper; he will be highly exalted.
But many were amazed then they saw him. His face
was so disfigured he seemed hardly human, and from his
appearance, one would scarcely know he was a man. And
He will startle many nations. Kings will stand speechless
in his presence. For they will see what they had not been
told; they will understand what they had not heard about"
(Isaiah 52:13-15 NLT).

Startled nations in Bethlehem—
Three wise men, shepherds stood speechless.
They saw and understood
Amazed highly Exalted One
Came as a baby—
Returning in holy light,
You startled Paul on Damascus road;
You startled hell when You descended and took the keys, set captives free,
Swallowed up death—
Shot through realms of the Spirit—*dunamis* explosion,
Resurrection's power.
Keys—sound of the keys of authority,
The Lion who's the Lamb,
Baby in a manger with sheep,
Shepherd—perfect Lamb,
No keys in His tiny fingers.

He was the key and the door
To eternal life;
He gave Himself willingly.
No man took His life.
He unlocked death, hell, and the grave;

Donna Milham

Jesus—baby in a manger,
Eternal eyes,
Beautiful baby,
Unrecognizable on the cross,
Beautiful in resurrection,
Glorious in His return.

Eternity's Pulse of Worship

Psalms 104:1-2

"O Lord, my God, Your greatness takes my breath away.
Overwhelming me by Your majesty, beauty, and splendor!
You wrap Yourself with a shimmering, glistening light!"

You took off this robe, stepped out of heaven,
Stepped into the womb of a handmaiden,
The cry on her lips still echoing upon earth.
Angels carried her response to heaven;
It echoed there.
The stars resounded in brilliant light—
The Father rejoiced.
Salvation's plan has begun this day,
Heaven's response to an open womb—a holy yes,
A laid down life,
He took off His robe of light and became a seed
And stepped into her womb.
Eternal Son, a seed,
The seed of promise for all of man's destinies;
Father rejoiced, for His children would be His again.

But the Son is gone from heaven;
I wonder, what was it like
When He vacated His heavenly home?
Angels watching,
Holy Spirit hovering over Mary
Even as He did at the command,
Let there be light.
From light Himself—Father of Lights—
Now Son of light within a woman's womb.
John leaped in Elizabeth's womb,
Recognized this Shining One,

Donna Milham

Whom he would make the way for,
Making way for the King of Kings.

Humility abounded that day, causing an eternal display
To pour into hearts for each test of pride and self-focus
To gaze upon and fall on our knees,
Crying—only Your will and Your way!

I wonder. Did the light within
Shine from His eyes,
Flashes of lightning escaping here and there,
Brilliant in what they carried from home?
The seed had within Himself all of heaven,
Totally dependent on Father and Spirit.

Holy Three—separated yet still one,
Showing the way to walk in union and dependency.
This robe of light,
Brilliant, dazzling with eternity's pulse of worship;
You are light—to earth and the heavens,
Bright morning star
Who awakens the dawn.

Sound of the Immortal Seed Within

Luke 2

The angel of the Lord appears to shepherds in a field
Outside of their village who were guarding their sheep.
They were doing what they did each day when a "suddenly" took place.
They were very close to where a miracle had just taken place,
Yet without a visitation would not have known the Messiah was born,
Close and yet so far.
The lost around us—He's at hand
Yet they do not see, do not know He has come;
Angel messengers,
Sons of light, messengers of good news, of great joy:
Behold, the Light has come—the Light of the World.

You will know Him—how?
Find Him in a manger, wrapped snugly in strips of cloth,
Humble clothing.
This One who left a robe of light,
Now wrapped in simple strips of cloth.
You will not find a great conquering king,
You will gaze upon love itself—
Perfect obedience,
Perfect love
Of Son for His Father.
His yes made way for our chance to also respond
To love's request for our hearts;
They would gaze at perfect love.
His cry resounded in heaven;
Did angels dance?
For the voice of the second person of the Trinity was heard once again.
For those nine months, what did it sound like without the voice of the Son?
Did His heartbeat in Mary's womb echo there?

114

Did it continue to be the rhythm of heaven?
The simple shepherds now surrounded with
Heaven's prophetic song
Sung by the armies of heaven,
For they knew their Commander,
Though a babe, was still the Lord of Hosts.
They prophesied heaven's song to earth:
"Glory to God in the highest realms of heaven!
For there is peace and a good hope given to the sons of men" (Luke 2:14).
Favored Mary, favored shepherds, favored Joseph.

Holy Spirit infilling
John the Baptist even before his birth;
No limitations—who can tell God what to do?
This baptism of fire from above,
This fire, this presence that was above and around the Israelites.

"God spread out a cloud as shade for them as they moved ahead,
And a cloud of fire to light up their night" (Psalm 105:39).

This fire now within Elizabeth's womb, within this child yet to be born;
He would come forth and be a blazing torch in the hand of God,
Set apart with words of truth, burning passion,
Preparing the way for the Bridegroom,
A true friend—friend of holy fire.

Oh, hear the sound—the sound of Mary greeting Elizabeth;
John leaped within
And then Elizabeth was filled with Holy Spirit,
And she prophesied of what she could not—did not—know:

"The moment you came in the door and greeted me, my baby danced
inside me with ecstatic joy! Great favor is upon you, for you have believed
every word spoken to you from the Lord" (Luke 1:44-45).

Jesus, a seed in Mary's womb,
Caused Elizabeth to bow in her heart and release prophetic decrees.
As a seed—divine seed of heaven—
She took a lowly posture and declared before His birth;
Her eyes opened—her heart understood by Spirit revelation.

Filled with the Spirit,
Her baby jumped for joy, danced with heaven's delight
Even as all creation would at His birth.
Do we hear the sound of Mary's greeting?
What did she say?
It still echoes in time.

The Lord sent her to Elizabeth
To help settle and seal within her, with another on earth
One who saw and heard, they would stand and believe together
When man did not understand
Impregnated by God.
Mary would not only remember Gabriel's visit,
But their face-to-face on earth visitation together
She would remember—John's leap,
Holy Spirit filling Elizabeth and her decrees over Mary.
She had no tape recorder or scribe to pen it down;
It was penned by Holy Spirit on her heart,
Finger of fire,
Writing it and we read it today—to remember,
She would remember entering the house and greeting this other
Chosen womb.
It would be a candid shot in her mind's eye and spirit
To call upon again and again
In the face of rejection, persecution, hard journeys, no room in the inn.
This moment, penned by His hand on the tablet of her heart,
Forever branded on her spirit.
Oh, Lord, brand us with holy revelation

That in darkest hours we remember
Sounds, leaps in wombs, decrees, and we press in.

"For through the eternal and living Word of God you have been born
again. And this 'seed' that he planted within you can never be destroyed
but will live and grow inside of you forever" (1 Peter 1:23).

The holy seed sperm—Jesus Himself put now within us;
No longer mere mortals, we are a race that has never existed before—
Sons of God,
Holy because He is holy.
As He increases in us through our daily dying, daily communion,
We decrease.
This immortal Eternal Lord—the Word
Within us.
Be holy for I am holy.
Mary's womb—our wombs,
Not tombs of hopelessness and despair,
As are the lost without Jesus,
As were we before this salvation.
This seed going in—born again into eternal future and hope,
We yield ever more to Him.
We must see—meditate on—
We are not just men but sons of God.
Little gods
Made in His image,
Not meant for just the ordinary,
But the extraordinary,
Supernatural realms of God.
He wants us to carry Him and birth His purposes—
Noble purposes, holy purposes—
See ourselves as He sees us;
We are foreigners in this world,

We do not fit,
Never meant to fit,
We are His offspring.
He did not come into this world to fit in but to transform,
To bring the kingdom of heaven to earth,
To reveal Father—His home—our true destiny,

Immortal seed within us.
What does this look like?
What comes forth from our lives—this seed within you?
Our DNA is from the Holy Three.
We must not focus on our earthly father's or mother's DNA
With weakness, failures, and generational things,
But on our holy heritage and line—
Christ Jesus in us.
Regenerated, truly born again, fully alive,
No lack—to live and move and have our being in Him
Because He is in us and we are in Him,
Clothed within with light—
Pulsating light, wanting to get out.
Let there be, let there be, let there be
Pushing at gates of our lives
Mouths, eyes, hands, feet, hearts, ears,
Holy declarations of life-giving light and life
Pushing at gates—let us out!
Be releasers of holy life,
It is not for the one next to you,
It is you—young and old this day,
Immortal seed within.
Do you see it?
Will you carry Him?
Holy ark—holy wombs
Feel Him leap within you,
Leap of divine justice,
Waiting to be released through kingdom sons,

Donna Milham

Extending Him out of the gates of our lives.
Let the river flow out,
River of fire and life,
See it rushing forth—holy light
Consuming darkness.
You see injustice and release from the gates of life—womb
Justice, justice, justice, justice, justice,
Five piercings of justice on the cross
Now risen—in you and in me.

Chapter Ten: The Sound of New Creation

Can You Hear the Sound of a New Man—A New Race?

Truly owning—our old man is crucified,
New creation, new man, new order,
Birth out of His pierced side
With light, power, authority, joy, compassion,
Birth with His DNA,
We are brand new.
Crush every lie that says we are not
Born again from above;
Live as we truly are—truth.
Wasted time and battles, trying to resurrect the old man:
He is gone—dead on the cross—we are a new creation.
The great lie—first Adam is alive in us—no!
The great truth—second Adam is alive in us!
Hear the sound of new creation
Rising out of life—
Washing off the vomit and filth of demonic hordes,
Riding up the mountain of worship and declaration.

Second Adam
Firstborn of many—brother, King, new creation,
Sons of God—brides,
No shuffling of feet or eyes to the ground,
No murmuring, complaining, or comparing.
Holy declarations, holy joy, holy battles,
Beaten, shipwrecked, hungry, cold,
Victorious, satisfied, destiny, His dreams fulfilled,
Reward of His sacrifice,
Praises rise—I will arise.

Sound of unity (conversations, songs, feet in unison)
Lies, envy, inferiority, shame, compromise, comparison, jealousy
Swallowed up in the truth of who we are.

Sound of courage—declarations, firm steps, drums, hearts
Moving forth, unstoppable,
Able to scale a wall, leap over a troop
We are a new creation army—already dead.
Death has no hold on us!
Conquered at the cross and the resurrection—
Now conquered in us,
Death has no hold on me.
Resurrection reality—
New man, new creation—
Never existed before;
Jesus loosed them from this grip and into resurrection reality,
Now, today—enter anew.

The Enemy's greatest victory—if he can't get us into hell eternally—
Then to have us live on earth in the first Adam's fall
And not the second Adam's victory.

They came to David's cave distressed, disillusioned, in debt
And came out changed, transformed, filled with courage,
Able to kill 500, 600 lions in pits.
We enter into Galatians 2:20—death to self,
And come out in the power of His resurrection,
The other side of the cross
With all of the power of the sound of His majestic authority.

Hear the sound of authority—
New creation, redeeming, governmental authority
Decreeing mandates;
Heaven backs up its sons echoing their King.

Hear the sound of creativity—
New sound—new song
Speaking things into existence,
Sons—multiplying food,
Disaster response—going forth with healing.

"Christ lives in you. This gives you assurance of sharing his
glory."(Colossians 1:27 NLT).
Can you hear the sound of Christ in you?
Let Me out, let Me out
Holy fire, holy flames, holy burning,
Sound of victory,
Sound of intercession—tears,
Sound of war cries,
Sound of freedom.

We are in Him and He is in us;
We carry Him everywhere we go,
Pregnant with divine possibilities,
Filled with *dunamis* power.
We cannot, do not, dare any longer to walk in two worlds.
We must choose whose kingdom we fully belong to
And live fully in that kingdom.

Silence in the Garden

Silence in the garden
What was once
Laughter, joy, face-to-face communion
With the Creator,
Now silent.
Heaven is stunned,
Angels watch,
Father's heart broken,
Trinity's pain—
They can do nothing.

Heaven responds;
One evacuates heaven to seek the ones they long for.
He became one of us—became flesh and blood.
The Father communed again with this created being,
His Son,
Second of the Trinity made flesh,
Walked among us.
He revealed heaven on earth;
Emotions of the Trinity,
Longing and desire—
Oh, Jerusalem, Jerusalem, how I long,
He wrote in the sand,
He cried at the tomb,
He cared for His mother at the cross,
He revealed desire for divine relationship with the ones He created.

Are our gardens silent?
Did not Mary think at Jesus' tomb that it was the gardener?
When her eyes were opened—her response
To cling to Him;
She could not—not yet;
Holy intimacy with the One in the garden.

Donna Milham

What does heaven hear and see?
Are our gardens silent?
Will we walk with Him and talk with Him,
Commune and love Him in our gardens?
He is waiting for you and me
There.
Hell loves the silence;
Heaven waits,
Postures itself to hear the slightest whisper
Of a heart of devotion
For the One
Who is love
And will never stop loving us,
Who created us from within His heart.
Holy desire—
How He longs for you and me.
He waits.
Will we keep Him waiting or will be run into His arms?

Can You Hear the Sound of Goodness and Mercy?

Can you hear the sound of His goodness and mercy following you,
       Pursuing you, chasing after you?
Stop and look again over your shoulder.
It is not the enemy pursuing you—no.
Turn fully and look with wide-open eyes and heart.
It is His goodness and His mercy
All the days of your life,
Not some days or moments
But all of your days, 24/7/365.
Can you hear the sound of mercy that triumphs over judgment?
Judgment of yourself, of others,
The Enemy swallowed up, consumed, overtaken
In the sound of mercy.
Hear the sound of fresh beginnings,
Jump into His goodness and His glory!
       Splash in it, dance in it,
       Twirl in it, get lost in it,
Let it overtake you, stay right there in it until you are totally saturated in
The DNA of His glory—within, without, around,
Surrounding glory, goodness, mercy!
Can you hear the sound of holy feet
       Running into and running out with His glory?
In and out and in and out into His realms—His holy realms of glory—
Basking, waiting, transforming and going out into the world,
Releasing sounds of His goodness and mercy
Like the cloud over Peter—over you, in you,
Overtaking ones with divine appointments.
Who is this? What is this?
It's the sound of goodness and mercy
Overtaking lies, confusion, darkness, hopelessness, lack, despair—
See the realms of goodness and mercy manifest in the eyes and

126

Donna Milham

On the faces of His sons and daughters,
Called by His name who have dared to enter into the sounds of heaven and
Release the reality of those realms from holy encounter,
Release from their spirits the cry and prayers
Of the heart of the Son of God—
On earth as it is in heaven.
Can you hear the sound of goodness and mercy?
Release it—keep it not to yourself!
Release it—again and again and again!
There are those desperately needing to hear its sound so they can respond!
Be the sound of mercy and goodness on earth
As it is in heaven!

Do You Hear the Sound of a Door Open: Come Up Here?

The Enemy of your soul will tell you—that's for others.
This is the same voice that whispers to us in challenging times—
Where is your God?
All of His sons are to see in the spirit, live in the spirit, hear in the spirit.
Why? So we can be with Him and see, hear, and release heaven on earth.
Spiritual seekers go to the second heaven
And receive false hopes and promises;
The eternal invitation has been given to God's sons—
Come to the third heaven and receive Revelation,
Appropriate it deep within and become releasers of transformation.
One song—holy, holy, holy—
Can transform a city because it releases angels who are waiting
To go with swords of light into a city and dispel darkness.
One stroke of lightning on a painter's canvas
Pierces the darkness—will you?
Oh, may we hear it and see it and release it!
One beat of the drum releases thunder and the beat of the Father's heart,
And the choreography of heaven begins,
The dance of the angels of heaven with those on earth
Decreeing with sound and movement—worthy, worthy, worthy—
All woven together
Dispels the false voices—where is your God? Who is your God?
From these revelatory realms we release fresh new sounds
Eternal and now—holy, holy, holy—
A people of His presence,
Come up here, again and again and again,
Personally invited by the Father above.

Chapter Eleven: The Sound of Forgiveness

Breathe Out, Breathe In—Can You Hear the Sound of His Breath?

Jesus breathed out—exhaled

Forgiveness to His persecutors,

The ones who tried Him, killed Him, abandoned Him,

Denied Him.

He breathed out love and released a standard for all of time—

The cross—total forgiveness,

The test of true love.

Whether you ever hear the words, "I'm sorry,"

He never did, hanging on Calvary.

Whether things are ever made right this side of eternity or not,

His love *in us* breathes out,

"Father, forgive them,

For they don't know what they're doing" (Luke 23:34).

Breathe out the poison of bitterness;

Breathe in heaven's atmosphere of mercy.

Breathe out revenge;

Breathe in God's justice against injustices.

Breathe out false accusations;

Your accusers may not know the truth, but God does, so

Breathe in His delight, acceptance, and His truth.

Breathe out anger and breathe in peace!

Can You Hear the Sound of Forgiveness?

"God said to me, once and for all,
'All the strength and power you need flows from Me!'
And again I heard it clearly said,
'All the love you need is found in Me!' And He said,
'The greater your passion for more—
The greater the reward I will give you!'" (Psalm 62:11-12).

I believe that the Lord is calling out to us His people
And asking us to shift atmospheres with the Love of God.
I believe there is a divine access being given in this hour
To the lovers of God,
Access to sounds and realms
And heaven's kingdom authority and power that will
Release a sound that all of earth is awaiting—
Releasing the sound of forgiveness.

God is after every place of unforgiveness in our lives—
  Every wound,
  Every hidden place,
  Every place we have said or say we cannot forgive,
  That the individuals do not deserve to be forgiven.

Our DNA is love because He is love;
  We can choose to forgive,
  We can choose to love,
  We don't have to trust them again, but we must love and forgive.

We can be healing the sick, raising the dead, but if we don't have love and
forgiveness—Forgiving all—then we are not walking in what God has
called us to walk in—love.
Our call is to become sacrificial, laid down lovers—our lives fully His.

130

Donna Milham

This may seem impossible—
But it is possible because Jesus said it was and is.

Think of all of the followers of Jesus who had to forgive—
Saul who became Paul.
All of the fathers, mothers, and children,
Separated, jailed, martyred because of their faith.
Think of all of the cries in the night that they would hear,
Knowing they would never see their loved ones again
As they were arrested and
Taken away from their homes and families.

They chose to forgive and embrace this man as brother,
Then leader, then apostle.
This was the love of God in them and through them.
It would be humanly impossible otherwise.

These ones were scattered by persecution
But the end result was "uncontainable joy filling the city!" (Acts 8:8).
When they went to other cities they did not go in self-pity or gloom
But sharing and revealing the wonderful news of the Anointed One.

Many would be martyred.
Stephen was one of these—
Let us step into his final moments on earth together.

Hear the sound of love and forgiveness—
Let it open our eyes and ears afresh and anew.
Let these verses never be commonplace,
But be foundation stones for our walks as followers of Jesus.

"But Stephen was overtaken with great faith,
Was full of the Holy Spirit" (Acts 7:54).
Here was one who spoke to his fellow Jews and fathers,

Sharing of their history and of Jesus.
By the Spirit he spoke with great courage and conviction.

His gaze was fixed into the heavenly realm.
He was here and there at the same time.
As he spoke, he was living from being seated in heavenly places.
Here he heard and saw the Father, Son, and Spirit—
Heard angel songs and sounds of heaven—
From being and seeing into the realms
Of the One he worshiped, lived, and would die for.
He was living in a realm of supernatural love.

He saw the glory splendor of the Father.
He saw Jesus stand up at the right hand of the Father—
Jesus standing for one who was fully His,
Who looked and sounded like Him—
A son of God.
All of heaven watched and waited—
What would be Stephen's final actions in the moments ahead?

Can you hear the sounds of heaven?
I wonder. Was heaven silenced in these moments
As the great cloud of witnesses watched?
I wonder what it sounds like when the One who is the Lord of all stands?

Does everything and everyone bow?
Does the song of heaven escalate?
Do the archangels change their stance?

Hear the sound of one who is captivated,
Captured by the One he loves, lives for,
And is willing to lay down his life for.
        "Look"—this was not a wimpy decree or a slight whisper.
        No—a cry, a shout:
                "Look" (Acts 7:56)!

An announcer of what he is seeing—the reality of the kingdom of God—
More real than the earthly realm.

> "I can see the heavens opening" (Acts 7:56).
> Jesus stood—He opens the heavens,
> For He is Jacob's ladder, stairway, access
> To the Father and to His heavenly home.
> He stands—His gaze is fixed on Stephen,
> Their eyes locked in holy love

This is not the honor of man and man's kingdoms on earth,
This is Jesus Himself who hung on the cross
And looked into the eyes of His enemies,
His betrayers, who did not see the eyes of eleven of His disciples—
Only one and his mother and other women.
This is the One who knew what it was to be totally alone and He stood
And in His standing He kept His promise—
> "I will never leave you alone, never!" (Hebrews 13:5).

"The Son of Man standing at the right hand of God to welcome me
home!" (Acts 7:56).

What did this sound like, look like?
It was holy covenantal love in action in full display.

I believe Jesus' eyes were flashing with fiery, jealous love.
I believe the Father's heartbeat with His resounding rhythm that beats
within the heart of Jesus Echoed in Stephen's heart—
The Father's heartbeat of eternal love
Had been deposited within Stephen's heart.

He lived and walked in the rhythm of the Lion and the Lamb,
A servant who carried the power of the wonders of the love of heaven—
And he displayed it on earth.

It had been settled deep within him—
      My life is truly not my own;
      I have been bought with a price, the most
      Costly of sacrifices;
      The Lamb will receive His honor and His reward
      All of my love,
          All of my life,
              Nothing held back.

I will love as He does, for He is alive in me.
Hell—hear the sound of eternal love pouring through my being.

His blood, His love, my DNA is His.
Hear its rushing, surging sound, washing in me and through me.
It cleanses every false heart motivation,
Rips off the walls of my heart's memories—
      Yesterday's pictures of failure, rejection, wounds—
      And infuses holy sacrificial love from above, within.
Hear its sound as it surges into my soul and emotions,
      Filling me with His nature, His very self,
      Love, patience, kindness, gentleness, forgiveness, mercy—
      Supernatural holy love, light, and life—washing in and through,
      Taking my heart by storm as I surrender—
      Love's captive, a prisoner of love;
      Hear the sound of perfect liberty—
      God's perfect love casts out all fear.

No one else may see this—
Stephen is amongst a crowd and yet alone in heaven's spotlight;
A drama of the ages is at hand—what will be the final scene?

The sound of heaven—
The crowd cannot bear it.

"His accusers covered their ears with their hands
And screamed at the top of their lungs to drown out his voice" (Acts 7:57).

They didn't whisper,
They screamed at the top of their lungs to drown out Stephen's voice!

I believe his voice was supernaturally charged—
Like a trumpet that announced the truth of another realm.
They covered their ears,
      Choosing to be deaf and silence truth again.
      They tried to shout louder to drown him out,
But heaven will not be silenced.

"Look!" Stephen said, " I can see the heavens opening" (Acts 7:56).
Stephen was announcing the King of Glory
His voice trumpeted truth, reality, resurrection reality—
He's alive; He's conquered death, hell, and the grave;
And His victory is in full display!
He stands for me;
I am not afraid, my true home welcomes me.

Does the community we live in, the people around us,
Hear this sound in our lives?
The sound of holy love—the sound of decrees of truth—
From holy encounters with our King?

They could not stand it for one minute longer—
They could not silence Stephen,
They could not drown him out;
Heaven cannot be drowned out
By hands over man's ears or by man's shouts.

"Then they pounced on him and threw him outside the city walls to stone
him" (Acts 7:58).
Hear the sound of anger, self-righteousness, religion, murder;

Can You Hear the Sound?

See their eyes of hatred and despising;
Hear the sound of a mob gone wild with demonic frenzy—
Men clamoring over each other, pulling,
Dragging Stephen this way and that,
Probably hitting, spitting on him as they did to Jesus.
Were there shouts—stone him, kill him—
Similar to what they shouted over Jesus—crucify Him?

The angels watched as they did that day of Jesus' crucifixion.
They were not released to do anything but watch.
In a moment 10,000 angels would, could be there—
But this man's life was to be given in love's surrender
And would release miracle seeds—
Seeds and sounds that would release transformation.

"His accusers, one by one,
Placed their outer garments at the feet of the young man
Named Saul of Tarsus" (Acts 7:58).
At his feet—what a contradiction—
Mary at Jesus' feet, kissing and washing the feet of the One
Who would soon have His feet pierced for her sins—
Feet that would be victorious in resurrection's love and power.

Here these soon-to-be murderers lay their garments
At their murderous leader Saul's feet.

Can you see this—hear this?
As one by one they purposely chose—
Came forward in full view for all to see—
To be counted and recognized
As ones who would gladly stone and kill Stephen.

Can you hear the sounds of hell
Celebrating what they think this demonic murderous mob will soon
Release into hell's chambers—another soul.

There is a spiritual atmosphere of two kingdoms colliding—
      Heaven and hell,
      Light and darkness;
Both have sounds—one will overtake the other.
Our actions, responses, decrees help decide
Which kingdom's sound overtakes, defeats,
Conquers the other in the situations we are in and face each day.

"As they hurled stone after stone at him" (Acts 7:59).
Can you hear the sound of stone after stone hurled?
Can you hear the grunts of the men as they throw with all of their might?
      This wasn't skipping a pebble across a lake or seashore,
      This was murder—hell's release on earth—
      Violent and without mercy.
      One after the next, man after man, stone after stone.
Hell roared with the sound of each stone hurled—
A rhythm of hell's dance revealed and
      Released on earth.

Heaven watched as stone after stone landed upon its victim—
      But Stephen was a prisoner of love
      And each stone became an altar of worship
      And loving sacrifice
      Releasing a Galatians 2:20, Philippians 3:10 sound
      Of a life not my own
      Of the fellowship of His sufferings
      And the power of His resurrection.

Sounds of the eternal now in full display.
Hear the sound of Father, the Son, and Holy Spirit through Stephen—
      Sound of eternal forgiveness,
      Sound of the blood of Jesus,
      Sound of mercy,
      Sound of the Lion and the Lamb.

Can You Hear the Sound?

I believe this was not a whisper;
I believe it was a trumpet shout,
As the stones impacted his earthly body,
His spirit man cries out through his parched lips—

"Our Lord Jesus, accept my spirit into your presence" (Acts 7:59).

Can you hear and see the mob is even angrier?
Still they cannot silence what they think is insanity and blasphemy;
They haul more stones—how many, how long?

Amazingly up to this point Stephen is standing.
Jesus is standing and Stephen is standing, eye to eye,
Face to face, heart to heart.

Heaven and earth kiss in holy adoration,
Heaven's ruling King of an army of angels is standing in full array,
And the one who looks and sounds like Him—
Who echoes the very voice and
Cry of the One he loves—is looking straight into His eyes.

"Then he crumpled to his knees" (Acts 7:60).
The stones are now destroying his earthly home—
It gives way under the crush
And blow of the endless barrage of hurling stones,
But the sound of holy surrender overtakes
The sounds of murder and hatred.

I believe as each stone hit his earthly temple,
A song and sound rose within his heart of worship and adoration—
To be counted worthy to be called His own
I wonder with each stone did he cry—holy, worthy?
Did it echo with the rhythm of the eternal song?

Donna Milham

"Holy, holy, holy is the Lord God, the Almighty—
    The one who always was, who is,
    And who is still to come" (Revelation 4:8 NLT).

    "You are worthy O Lord our God,
    To receive glory and honor and power" (Revelation 4:11 NLT).

"Then he crumpled to his knees and shouted in a loud voice" (Acts 7:60).
This is supernatural—he has fallen to his knees—
    The place of worship, adoration with shouts and trumpets.

"Our Lord, don't hold this sin against them" (Acts 7:60).
Hear the sound of forgiveness echoing through time and space;
It meets in the realms of eternity—the echo of Jesus' cry on the cross.

    "Father, forgive them, for they know don't know
    What they're doing" (Luke 23:34).

These words meet with a holy kiss in the Spirit
And release the atmosphere of
Heaven's explosive light—
Light overtakes darkness.
Angels escort Stephen home as he dies and lives now forevermore.

Heaven is welcoming, angels stand in awe,
The audience of those gone before him wait with a holy embrace.

He had become like the One he loved—
The very substance of love encompassed his life.
    "And they have defeated him by the blood of the Lamb
    And by their testimony.
    And they did not love their lives so much
    That they were afraid to die" (Revelation 12:11 NLT).

"Now, Saul agreed to be an accomplice to Stephen's stoning
And participated in his execution" (Acts 8:1).

Hell thought it had won,
Saul thought he had won,
The false sound of a false victory—
        The sound of deception, darkness, and eternal damnation.

The sound of forgiveness echoes through time and space,
        Comes to us in moments we need to choose to love, to forgive,
                And to release mercy.

Will heaven in us silence hell's cry around us?
        Be bitter—
        How can you forgive?
        I will never forgive them,
        Vengeance is my right,
        They deserve to pay,
        You don't understand what they did.
        Revenge, I simply want revenge,
        Silent seething deep within.

Will the seed of our lives and response to heaven's cry
Bring forth Sauls transformed to Pauls?

Saul was full of angry threats, rage,
Wanting to murder the disciples of Jesus.
He had received authority and letters
From the high priest and the religious leaders.
Religious spirits were leading the dance of murder and persecution
To arrest followers of the way.

Saul wanted to capture and arrest all of the believers;
His passion was persecuting the church.

"So he obtained the authorization and left for Damascus. Just outside the city, a brilliant light flashing from heaven suddenly exploded all around him" (Acts 9:3).

Light, sounds, suddenlies of God.
"Falling to the ground, he heard a booming voice say to him,
'Saul, Saul, why are you persecuting me?'" (Acts 9:4).
The sound of the King Eternal,
Crying out from His same eternal heart posture
And echoing afresh with his martyred, loved Stephen—forgive.

"The men accompanying Saul were stunned and speechless" (Acts 9:7).
These were not wimpy men, but men on a mission from hell,
Filled with anger and rage—
They were stunned and speechless—at what?

"For they heard a heavenly voice but could see no one" (Acts 9:7).

"Who are you, Lord?" (Acts 9:5).

"I am Jesus, the Victorious, the one you are persecuting.
Now, get up and go into the city, where you will be told
What you are to do" (Acts 9:5-6).

If we love, it is because of His love within;
If we don't forgive, we hold ourselves captive—
    Not prisoners of love but of hurts, pain, and the past,
    We hold others prisoners with our unforgiving hearts.

Ears once deaf, now hear.
Eyes that once saw, now are blind in the natural,
    But the eyes of the heart and spirit are open.
Saul to Paul,
    Who would one day call himself the chief of sinners,
    Yet walking fully as a son in His amazing love.

Can You Hear the Sound?

Saul had to forgive himself—
He had to receive forgiveness
From all of the families he had been used to destroy.

The sound of forgiveness, the fruit of forgiveness
        Releases slaves from hell's captivity,
        Releases into future and hope.
        Hope's sound is founded upon the sound of forgiveness.

Our hope was founded at His cry of, "Father forgive them!"

Now we are able to live in the cry of the second and final Adam,
        Firstborn Son of many sons to come forth,
        Birthed from the heart of love—the Father's heart
        To bring forth the sounds and songs of the realm
        Of His kingdom on earth.

The sound of forgiveness releases us,
        Releases others,
        Releases hope and mercy.

Sound of prisoners of love—
        No longer slaves to the past,
        To wrongs done to us or through us.
        Perfect love casts out all fear.

"But love's perfection drives the fear of punishment
Far from our hearts" (1 John 4:18).
"Dispenses his life into mine (Galatians 2:20).
Now we can become atmosphere changers with the love of God.

We are told by the Lord to love our enemies—even the Sauls in our lives.
Saul, who sought to arrest and kill the believers of his day, a terrorist,
Would hear words he never dreamed possible.
They are words of another kingdom

That have overtaken the heart of a lover of God—
               "Saul, my brother" (Acts 9:17).

What would we do today? What will we do today?

As we look back for a moment at Acts 7:54—
Stephen was overtaken with great faith;
        The people were overtaken with great rage.

The kingdom we serve is what overtakes us, our hearts, our thoughts.
Stephen was full of the Holy Spirit—
He fixed his gaze on the heavenly realm and saw glory.
This is what Jesus spoke to Nathaniel and to all of us—
The divine access given to all of the lovers of God;
Jesus is the ladder, the access to heaven.

His love pouring through Stephen, releasing forgiveness—
Disciples of love
Changing atmospheres with holy love.

Saul was there at Stephen's death—he held the cloaks of murderers—
But the atmosphere around his life was transformed
By a disciple of love releasing the sound of forgiveness.
Stephen was a seed in the ground—a seed of holy sacrificial love.
The response of heaven—
Saul's encounter with the One who stood for Stephen—
Birthed the apostle Paul; Saul was transformed to Paul.
Atmosphere changers—shifting destinies—eternally.

Atmosphere changers—
As we are faithful to walk in obedience to what God calls us to do
By faith in and through love.
Shifting atmospheres with His voice released through us,
With love, compassion, forgiveness,
We are His voice upon the earth.

Can You Hear the Sound?

He is within us—
We are His temple upon the earth
To carry His glory, His goodness, His love, His forgiveness.
The transforming power of the love of God is resident within our hearts.
We live within His love, flowing in and out and around—
Shifting atmospheres.

The sound of forgiveness—
      Stephen's, "Forgive them!"
      Sounded like Jesus,
      Sounded like the atmosphere of heaven;
      Jesus stood.

I believe He still stands for those whose lives are laid down,
Who carry and release this sound of "Father forgive them"—
True love, even unto death.

      The sound of hope—the sound of forgiveness.

Forgive them, Father—
      The sound of power,
      The sound of love,
      The sound of Father's heart.

Release the sound of forgiveness!

About the Author

Rev. Donna Milham is founder of Eagle & Dove Ministries. She is called as a leader to train, equip, and release others in living a Galatians 2:20 lifestyle. Her desire is for people to know the love of God the Father in an experiential way and to be established on the foundation of what His Word has to say regarding who they are in Christ.

She loves to lead others in the contemplative art of waiting on God and hearing His voice. Her heart's cry is to minister to the Lord and to give Him His heart's desire through a lifestyle of surrender, worship, and an abandoned heart. She has a passion for the Body to corporately encounter and minister to the Lord.

She believes it is the hour that God is calling us higher and deeper into the realm of holy encounters with the Lord. It is the hour of visitation, for the transformation of our hearts and lives, that we would walk with His divine nature deposited within our spirit—Christ in us the hope of glory. That this visitation would lead us further into the reality of being carriers of His glory, a place where He abides. From this place of abiding that we would bring His love, light, and life into the every sphere of influence as the Spirit of God leads us.

Donna is ordained by Rick Joyner's Morningstar Fellowship of Ministries, Ft. Mill, South Carolina.

Donna can be contacted at:

info@donnamilham.com
donnamilham@comcast.net

Websites:

www.donnamilham.com
www.eagledove.com

Made in United States
North Haven, CT
29 April 2024

51888735R10083